An Arab Awakening Tied to Arab Union's Formation

"**The book deals with** a high tech plan: an R&D-based techno-economic, educational, and industrial one. History teaches us that the plan had shifted numerous nations/regions from an underdeveloped to rich developed ones. They met their national dreams compared to others that failed to implement it, remaining as a result underdeveloped. This change is supported by numerous cases shown throughout the book whose goal is: to show these underdeveloped nations how to meet their nations/regions' dream by following and implementing it (the plan) routinely, on a steady, continuous basis.   A prime region that now fits this transformation is the Arab region; it has been selected in this proposal to illustrate the Arab awakening by the establishment of an "Arab Union" (AU) modeled after the 5 decades successfully operated "European Union" (EU). The proposal is further generalized to cover other geographies stagnant nations/regions ripe for advancement that have the determination and willpower to execute the plan."

By: Dr. Ata M. Hassan

Ata M. Hassan, Jr.

Blue Revolution Foundation, San Diego, California

....

T0105582

Order this book online at www.trafford.com
or email orders@trafford.com

Most Trafford titles are also available at major online book retailers.

Note for Librarians: A cataloguing record for this book is available from Library
and Archives Canada at www.collectionscanada.ca/amicus/index-e.html

Printed in Victoria, BC, Canada.

ISBN: 978-1-4269-2165-0

*Our mission is to efficiently provide the world's finest, most comprehensive book publishing
service, enabling every author to experience success. To find out how to publish your book, your
way, and have it available worldwide, visit us online at www.trafford.com*

Trafford rev. 2/03/2010

www.trafford.com

North America & international
toll-free: 1 888 232 4444 (USA & Canada)
phone: 250 383 6864 ♦ fax: 812 355 4082

Religions tell us all humans are created equal; they come to this life penniless and leave it equally without a penny. They are remembered only by their good work.

In life, however, they are divided into rich advanced and poor underdeveloped nations/ regions. For all those who are determined and willing to shift and transform their poor nations/regions status to rich or emerging one: read, follow and implement (free) the proposal as many other developing nations already did; they achieved their objective - satisfying their nations dream - and are now   successfully prosperous, rich nations although many were poor, some dominated by military junta and one party military rule.

To all such nations/regions which successfully already achieved the shift or others newly determined to undertake the formula's challenge - shift from developing to a developed techno-economic status - we freely present and contribute this book.

Acknowledgment

Thank you to my wife for her patience, encouragement, and assistance during the completion of this humane work.

Thank you to my beloved family now living in the United States, Europe, Palestine, Jordan, and various Middle Eastern countries – an international family whose concern is improving the world for all humanity, irrespective of their race or faith. Thank you also to my granddaughter and grandsons, Yasmine, Kareem and Rayan, for their help in preparing parts of this book.

Thank you also to others for their contribution in editing parts of the book including: Emeritus Professor John Joseph for his relevant review and suggestion on the history part - Chapters 1 and 5; Emeritus Professor Ben Oostdam and Mr. Ted A. Kuepper for their review of the R&D sections of this book, Chapters 2 through 4.

Contents

Preface

"Since the transition of the first humans from hunting and food gatherers to farmers followed by settling in villages and cities, the human race continued developing the earth and its resources to its current modern present state. Now, human society and the earth's population are divided into the have, rich, developed and, unfortunately, the have-not, poor, developing nations/regions. Throughout the ages, depending on political and economic technological planning and development, nations/ regions exchanged positions by being sometimes rich, prosperous, developed or poor, developing systems. The Arab world experienced such drastic change from having their Golden Rule Era (750-1300), pursuing knowledge and knowhow development, masters of their destiny in control over several centuries of a vast empire from Spain to the borders of China; declined dropping down to their present status of 20 contiguous but divided countries, majority (88%) are poor none coordinated, none cooperative, developing countries and population; incapable of neither developing themselves nor others, living with many conflicts and problems among themselves and foreign powers. The book message - the proposal - is how to awaken the Arab nations, bring them back to prosperous, rich region by copying and rigidly implementing what the neighbors "the European Union" have successfully done during the last 5 decades. The transformation is highly encouraged by the present local and foreign geopolitical and economical world situation. In addition one part of the Arab World is oil-rich has huge excess cash and all parts have the extensive land, the manpower and natural resources; all are supported by the present very strong relationship with its European neighbor. The proposal is further generalized and illustrated to cover other developed or developing nations that had taken the steps or others that are now determined and willing to pursue the proposal's approach".

The disastrous World War II, which caused the death of over 67 million humans, brought a lot of destruction and poverty to too many lands, led to changes in nation's political and techno-economic status and world order. For example, in Asia and Africa, all nations previously colonized by European or Japanese powers were set free and made independent, many of which were able during 5 decades to change their status from low and severe poverty, militarily dominated, to high tech progressive societies. Furthermore, post World War II era, all now advanced and emerging nations of the world - without exception- changed their economic planning. Presently they rigidly utilize "a highly effective, open market R&D-based techno-economic, educational and industrial plan that resulted in an improved economy, markets and highly developed status of these nations". In most cases, the plan was heavily supported and combined also with strong agricultural along with many other developmental efforts including that of social and health systems. Many countries main concern was redirected toward developing this important "techno-economic plan". Japan achieved high economic progress, now it is second world richest economy - in year 2006 - behind the number one, "The U.S.A". The European too, not only rigidly followed the above advanced nations techno-economic plan, but also tailored it to a complimentary new advanced, modern "European Union", replacing imperialism and super nationalism political and economic rule then was practiced during prewar period. The huge lands and massive populations of: Brazil, Russia, India and China (now known as **BRIC** countries' group) all are now pursuing more or less this same techno-economic advanced nations approach that yielded them the recently acquired - year 2007- high double digit growth economy. Contrary to these developed and emerging countries, many other world nations did not follow the aforementioned R&D-based techno-economic and educational approach and as a result were left behind, causing them post the war to remain until present day as developing nations, some with a limited degree of techno-economic development and others with none.

The Research and Development (R&D)–based techno-economic, educational transformation's formula as illustrated by the Arab Union case - to be referred to hereafter in the book as the proposal - is designed to assist the willing, determined but now underdeveloped nations/regions of the world catch up with advanced societies, delivering them from developing to developed status societies. In the past, the proposal's validity has been proven several times by many nations/regions that successfully carried it to successful completion. Consider for illustration the techno-economic and social welfare's concern of early governments of East Asia Pacific Ridge nations plus the European Union and many others countries in Europe and elsewhere: how they were and how they are now: by rigidly following this techno-economic plan- the proposal. They were able eventually to accomplish their goal of upgrading their then low performing, economically developing society to that of a highly successful, rich and prosperous, high tech society. The nations of South Korea, Singapore, Ireland and European Union (EN)'s region, were able by following the above techno-economic formula approach to raise their per capita GDP income in year 2007 to a very high GDP per capita of : $24,783, $49,714, $43,144 and $33,482, respectively, from where it was very low GDP income 5 decades back. In year 1961, South Korea had per capita GDP income of only $82, compared in same year to then a poor Singapore fishing village and Ireland was among the poorest country in Europe. Meanwhile, 17 now rich EU members, because of massive need following the disastrous World War II, received four years of the USA's Marshall's aid program - from 1947-195. These many nations were able, along with many others, to accomplish this transformation in spite of the many problems they faced, such as some had severe poverty and military rule. Such problems were positively dealt with and solved during the transformation process (for more detail, see Chapters 3 and 4). This phenomenon proved that only by nations' adoption of such above modern progressive R&D-based techno-economic can achieve a progressive, healthy economy.

The EU formation and development not only created a large, rich local European Economic Community Market replacing the old, weak fragmented imperial colonial markets but also gave the region the many great benefits as described in "Summary Section" of the book. The union although provided the region dominating world power, highly respected and admired by all nations, both the EU's population and governments are now very much concerned with other world nations' welfare and benefits, providing aid to many under privileged poor nations.

The above union and expanded market initiative made the EU the ideal model to be followed by many would-be prime candidate poor regions with the objective of changing their present developing case to a healthy, rich developed status. (They have, developed, advanced and have-not, developing, non-developed nations division was introduced by U.N. to distinguish between the two groups' rich and poor nations, particularly as relate to national techno-economic development). The model was selected as the proper model choice for the necessary, essential "Arab World Awakening": by the formation and development of an "Arab Union modeled after the European Union". The example was used throughout the book in order to demonstrate the aforementioned assumption and how it can be used to transform this developing region to that of a developed status case, provide it the same advantage as the model. The region's anticipated many benefits are summarized under the following "Summary Section" of the book. Similar union and model holds also true for all other nations/regions that are willing, determined and are highly concerned to shift from poor developing to developed status. For brevity, however, the transformation process will be limited to AU case, although the transformation process will be generalized to other suitable cases. The proposal's choice is strongly supported by the many promoting factors and stimuli together with the beneficial advantages gained by the Arab and other world regions are described in summary form in the following "Summary Section". Additionally, most important, and is in conformity with the EU model shall maintain each AU member country's independence, retaining the same form of government and being attentive to all present Arab governments demand, irrespective of being royalty or republics.

Problems facing the Arab world (equally facing other developing nations) are mainly economical in nature, requiring economical as well as industrial and political solutions to allow them to overlook their present petty disputes, which in many cases are driven by personal gain and extraneous conflicts. For ease, fast and appropriate AU formation, it is recommended that the Arab World should cultivate the present friendly relationship now existing between the two neighbors - EU and Arab regions - by seeking EU's aid as an advisor catalyzing the AU formation, just as it already recently (August, 2008) catalyzed the Arab-European "Union of the Mediterranean (UM)" nations.

The AU case success rests on the condition that the Arabs must agree to overlook - as the EU did - their differences. The AU's governments and population must also develop a compromising union building dialogue as was done too by EU. Living in the first 21ˢᵗ century with all its advances in various fields of economy and technology, the many open regional market unions and open trade agreements tell us now is the time for the Arab to unite and to stop continue quarrelling and arguing about petty problems; think of the region's future and population; compromise, coordinate and also seriously consider the great benefits that the region acquires by AU unity: the free open common market and the development of an advanced economy. The old techno-economic failure must be discarded and replaced by modern concepts as presented in the proposal.

The way we see it, Europe Union countries are now united, with many potential members anxiously waiting to join it: Ukraine, Turkey and others. Presently, EU countries are cooperating and coordinating economic and market condition with Russia. On the other hand, the United States and Canada are in full agreement, full cooperation and coordination in many national and international affair issues, nearly having a common united community's stance, with free trade and best of relations. Greater cooperation and binding agreements tie both with their North American region, Mexico. Brazil is now following both in development. The huge east Asia-Pacific region of over 1.5 billion population including China, Japan and the East Asia-Pacific Ridge countries - also Australia, New Zealand, and Turkey are now among some advanced or emerging nations with India pursuing them in advanced nation's techno-economic development. The above situation leaves Africa, the Spanish speaking South America, the Caribbean plus many countries in parts of Asia, especially Muslim and Arab countries, as non-developed nations in search of a Messiah or a techno-economic prophet to lead them out of their present developing status to that of a developed one!

Now, with the financial and economic crisis presently confronted the world since mid year 2008, the advanced nations rose to the occasion by having their coordinated G8, G7 and EU Summits, followed by the G20 wealthiest nations' continuing and coordination Summits, pledging cooperation and huge bailout sum of capital to confront the financial and economic crisis. The bailout process was extended recently wherein the rich EU member country leaders approved increasing bailout aid to Eastern European EU ex-communist members to 100 billion euro. The very recent 20 nations Summit in London, April 2009, pledged $1.1 Trillion global bailout to revive world trade and economy.   The 20 Arab World countries had their joint Summit Arab Economic Conference in Kuwait (January 2009) to deal among other subjects with the present financial and economic crisis. By contrast to the above, no collective cooperative funding or bailout aid, however, was made by many other developing, struggling countries. Now: who shall look after these developing, struggling nations with their massive human population? In the past the G8 pledged under the U.N. Millennium Development Goals (MDG) program to help the poorest nations overcome their poverty but fail to completely deliver the promised aid (see Chapter2). During the above 20 richest nations London and the G8 Italy Summits- held in presence of many other developing and emerging nations - they too pledged aid to these developing nations. Again, how effective this promised aid to the many developing and poor nation's remains to be seen!

There is only one way for these so far deprived, developing nations to pursue in reaching their techno-economic goal, i.e., the way which was followed and completed by South Korea, Singapore, Ireland and European Union, China, Brazil, Russia, India and of course U.S.A plus many other countries (see above). These many countries realized their **nations' dream** by strictly following and rigidly apply the above highly progressive, greatly rewarding R&D-based techno-economic, educational and industrial plan. The process is facilitated if the region possesses the transformation requirements – such as now the Arab and the South American Continent's Spanish speaking regions - allowing it to move from the present developing to emerging or developed status regions. The proposal plan- AU modeled on EU and its generalized case to other countries - is utilized throughout the text to illustrate and guide others 'how to advance and transfer them - nations/regions - from developing to developed status' by effectively using the **proposal's** approach, i.e., **R&D-based techno-economic, simultaneously supported, completely integrated, fully compatible with a developed educational and technology/ industrial, social and other developmental systems plan, as now rigidly and routinely used presently by all developed nations.** The proposed AU move shall also provide the Arabs' region an alternative source of income, by lifting up the region's wealth, giving it the power to offset volatility in price of oil and other raw unindustrialized materials and commodities. It shall also give the region the ability to contribute to world science and scholarship as their ancestors did in the past; an act which has been nearly neglected by recent Arab generation. **(Where there is a well there is way).**

...   .

Summary

Presently based on degree of development and industrial advancement, the nations of the world are divided into developed and developing group of nations; the latter with varying degrees of techno-economic development. Specifically, all Arab World countries' population are currently classified as underdeveloped nations although they are segmented into oil –rich nations with high per capita GDP incomes – some amongst the highest in the world – and relatively non-oil producing, poor countries; the ratio of this division- oil to non-oil producing countries- is about 31% to 69%, respectively. Taking into account the present war situation in Iraq and the relatively high population of Algiers compared to oil income, this ratio of rich to poor Arab countries' population deteriorates further down to the indeed surprising ratio of approximately about 12% versus 88%!

As already indicated under the proposal's Preface and throughout the text, all advanced and emerging nations, without exception, have implemented and strongly adhered to R&D –based techno –economic and industrial developmental plans, simultaneously integrated with matching educational, technological, industrial, agricultural, social, health plans and other advanced programs as well. Massive technology and well –defined, highly –focused R&D constitute the backbone to those advanced nations' techno –economic developmental and industrial plans. For their advancement, the R&D efforts are justifiable and necessarily made affordable, obligatory and essential as well, by all and every advanced or emerging regions/ nations. Research and development is required to develop, upgrade, and to innovate new products for their science and highly industrial economies and rich markets as well as their social and other many life requirements. Global spending on R&D, exceeded $1 trillion in 2006 with the vast majority of this figure invested by advanced nations. Use of R&D is expected to rise significantly to meet the demands of greatly expanding world populations and life problems. For example, the European Union projection is to increase R&D funding by all and each member from its current 1.84% of GDP to 3.0 % by the year 2010. South Korea's projection is to increase R&D spending to 5% of GDP by the year 2012 from its current 3% of GDP. Other advanced countries such as U.S., China, Japan plus many others are following a common pattern by increasing R&D spending as a ratio of their nations GDP. In all mentioned cases, the goal of R&D funding by private to government sectors is designed to reach a ratio of about 70% to 30%, as it is now the case in many advanced communities.

By contrast, developing countries fail to pursue the advanced nations' R&D plan, leading to the observed great differences in overall status between them and the advanced nation group. For example, amongst the Arab world's rich and poor, techno –economic plans are nearly void of R&D, industrialization and techno-economic development; having non-collective, non-cooperative approach toward Arab common market's development. All their efforts in the latter periods were insufficient to upgrade them to advanced nations' status. The region's efforts in R&D-based techno-economic plans continue to be limited in quantity, quality, and effectiveness contributing to the lack of improvement in the regions science, technology, industry and overall economic platforms. Currently, an insignificant portion of Arab nations' GDP, estimated at the very low value of about 0.2 percent, is spent on scientific and developmental research. This ratio compares in year 2007 to GDP's R&D investment ratios in the United States, Japan, Finland, Sweden and Israel of: 2.7%, 3.18%, 3.52%, 3.86% and 4.95%, respectively. The contribution to R&D by the private sector in the Arab region is also negligible. Absent too are the Arab foundations dedicated to R&D work; all the limited R&D efforts are government sponsored and funded.

Some recent, positive movements are being witnessed in the Kingdom of Saudi Arabia and UAE, but in spite of these forward steps, investment in R&D, technology and industrialization plans in both countries and rest of Arab world need to be fast –tracked to address the pressing needs of these issues within the region. These activities are also required to allow for both a critical catch –up with other advanced nations and also to give the region the ability to solve many of its severe financial, social and techno-economic problems. Overall, the R&D and industrial activities supported by an open free enterprise common market are also limited and in some countries are completely missing.

Undoubtedly and by far one of the greatest advancements and successful techno –economic plans achieved on a grand regional scale according to this approach, i.e., unity coupled with R&D –based techno –economic and industrial developmental plans and open common market, was the formation (1957) and gradual implementation over the last five decades of the "European Union (EU)". The present EU member countries have grown tremendously and are continuing to expand; now it has 31 member nations and over 500 million populations. Most recently, in August year 2008, the EU jointly with 10 Arab Mediterranean state they formed a separate union, the "Union of the Mediterranean Nations" with 43 member nations and over 756 million people, which constitute a separate union.

The founding of the European Union countries allowed Europe to depart from the harsh times, which culminated during World War II, to its current glorious rich status post EU establishment. Their progress was achieved in spite of EU countries having 26 different languages and numerous religious sects; also in spite of the region receiving then as reported -1947-1951- a required U.S.A. Marshall's aid program. Additionally, the union was made between the then rich developed Western and the relatively less rich and less developed South, Central and Eastern European nations. They were able to achieve this highly respected flourishing goal by using common sense and the justification and equally demonstrating of the many political and economic benefits that was gained by the founding of the European Union. The great success of EU was also achieved by the European's overlooking all their earlier disputes including the great very strong enmity of the very highly destructive World Wars I and II. Alone, the last war killed worldwide over 67 million persons, destroyed many countries, cities and lands. In addition, it induced both industrial destruction and population's poverty, qualifying Western and Southern Europe as indicated to receive the above US Marshal's aid program.

Besides uniting the region, improving the economy, advancing and developing both industry and technology, the founding of the EU is credited for bringing peace, unity and security to the region. The union provided the region with a huge and extensive open free enterprise market in addition to providing it with a strong stance in the face of the many presently dominating world powers. Now, the EU community is a major dominating world power, highly respected and admired by all nations, although still very much concerned with other world nations' welfare and benefits including providing aid to the poor nations.

The above proposal- transformation of nations/regions from developing to developed status - is not a steady state nor a scientific fiction phenomenon; rather it is a well proven approach which was not only successfully accomplished and fully proven by the above EU case alone and much earlier by U.S.A federation but also was equally well successfully proven by all the numerous nations regions that applied it. For example, the three countries given under "Preface Section" - South Korea, Singapore and Ireland- had during the early 1960s, about five decades ago, a considerably desperate, poverty stricken, very low GDP income. By leveraging structured R&D –based techno –economic and industrial developmental plans, they - the three countries - were able to transform their nations to highly developed high –tech industrial nations, with greatly improved GDP income per capita as was shown earlier in Preface Section. Singapore and Ireland now rank the 5th and 7th wealthiest per capita GDP nations worldwide, respectively (see Chapter2). Other emerging advanced nations of East Asia Pacific ridge nations such as Taiwan plus many others in Europe followed the same successful approach to transfer their nations from previously developing to developed nations' status. Also, Russia, Brazil, China and India, each with extensive land and huge population, followed the same developed nations' approach in planning their techno-economic plans; now - year 2007- they have high double digit growth economy (for more detail see Chapters 3 and 4). (Coincidentally, many Arab nations put forth economic plans during the same time period yet were nearly void of R&D and the outcomes have been far less fruitful).

The initiative AU modeled after EU was selected as the regional AU model (reasons for the selection are detailed in Chapter 6, Section 6.1) with the prime objective that the successful outcome is the transfer and upgrade Arab region's largely stagnant developing economy to an advanced economy status. Although other regions of the world could qualify for the transformation change, for brevity only the AU case shall be utilized here through out the book to illustrate the anticipated transformation change. Under the super friendly relationship now existing between the two neighbors, the European Union and Arab regions, especially when Europe discarded colonialism; the EU stands to aid the Arab region catalyze a speedy formation and development of the proposed AU, the same way it already recently catalyzed the formation of the "Union of Mediterranean (UM) Countries".

The AU Initiative is further supported by parts of the Arab region now has great capital wealth from the very expensive sale of oil and gas (see Chapter 2) plus potentially the region has skilled manpower - university graduates – plus abundant natural resources (see Chapter 1), that can be industrialized. This great wealth allows the region to start AU and to financially and technically operate it and overcome the hurdle and expenses of AU establishment and completion as well. The move is also strongly supported by the present major geopolitical and local techno –economical stimulus promoting and encouraging "Arab Union" formation and development (see Chapter 6, Section 6.4).

Founding of AU is anticipated to create a vast and open Arab common free enterprise market. The region is quite extensive, covers a huge region of land, about 13 million square kilometer; the 20 Arab countries are contiguous and centrally located; their land bordering two oceans and three large seas with a coastline in excess of about 23,000 km. Moreover, the AU initiative shall also create a large Arab consumer market's base of about 329 million residents in the region (year 2008); soon this number is expected to double within the upcoming two decades.

Let us remind the present Arab population - government and private sectors, especially the decision maker the government - that the founding and development of AU is not only relevant to present generation but more so to upcoming one. The future generation is growing at an alarming, spectacular birth rate. Their number is expected to double within the upcoming two decades. To make situation worst, the region is already suffering shortages in production of life-essential materials - water and food production - while the region's ratio of rich to poor now stands at only the meager value of 12% to 88%. All these facts make it essential for the Arab countries to quickly change their old techno-economic failure's plan, replacing it with AU modeled on EU formation.

"But would the present Arabs - governments under the pressure and high concern of private sectors - undertake the urgent responsibility to form and develop the proposed Arab Union modeled on European Union plan?"

The AU establishment is expected to provide the region the power to forget and overcome its past and now many characteristics present disputes over petty problems that led in the past as it does now too to many conflicts, sometimes to wars. The region's countries continue to suffer from many ridiculous wars now present in: Iraq, Palestine, 2006 war in Lebanon and previous Gulf wars, Iraqi-Iranian 8 year war as well as many other wars in various parts of the Arab region. Conflicts continue in other countries of the region: some in North African and other in parts of Arab Middle East countries and Sudan. Even Somali, the non-Arab Arab League's member, had its continuous local conflict for over 19 years. The formation of AU shall allow for peaceful, amicable solution to all disputes that may arise - local or with foreign powers - without having to resort to wars or major conflicts as was done in the past; AU shall deal with them the way its model EU deals now amicably with all conflicts.

To these above numerous advantages, the ultimate goals and major anticipated benefits - in summary form - of the present Arab Union proposal to the Arabs' population is the establishment within the region of:

- World –class R&D activity and funding with full regional development cooperation and coordination

- Educational programs simultaneously integrated with the R&D and other developmental activities

- Development of Arab technology with knowledge transfer to a strong industrial and economic base

- A common and free –enterprise huge market in the Arab region.

- Continues to maintain current form of government and each member country's independence

- Provides the region the extremely important, strong stance in the face of the many present and future geopolitical and economic conditions imposed on them by the dominating world powers, especially in presence of oil in the region. (This acquired stance compares to present weak one, where in many present occasions, because of lack of regional unity, the role and say of the Arab region was overlooked, many times totally ignored).

Extremely important, the formation of Arab Union shall also:

- Provides the region progress, improved living standards and an alternative source of income to offset future volatility in price of oil and other non- industrialized raw material commodities

- Establishes peace and security throughout the region, ending all its local and foreign conflicts and wars

- Gives the region the ability to contribute to world science and scholarship as their ancestors did in the past- "now completely neglected by the present Arab World"

- Very important, formation of AU shall stop the present drain of both the region's capital and brain's - scientists and other migrant manpower- wealth. Now the region is rated world number one in exporting wealth to advanced nations.

- The AU unity shall prevent foreign intruders waging wars and Arabs' land occupation, replacing them with greater trade and cooperation.

Details related to the proposed steps and approach to be undertaken to successfully implement the proposed "Arab Union" modeled on "European Union" are discussed in the book. As the relevance of R&D to the achievement of an advanced nation status is extremely critical to the advanced plan, three chapters of the book are dedicated to this subject while another section in a fourth chapter details the formation of the Arab Union with an emphasis on how to enhance R&D efforts in the region. Chapters in the book also describe how the 4 principles "Read, Write and perform R&D" were utilized by the Golden Age Arabs,750 to 1300, as they should be used by nowadays Arabs, to contribute to world knowledge and science (for detail see Chapter 5, Section 5.3.1).

The choice of the EU first as a model for the AU and second pursuing same EU steps in AU's implementation, made it first essential to provide strong evidence why EU was selected; second how to rigidly, successfully and perhaps easily and comfortably apply the same EU steps and approach in implementing AU's formation and development. The choice made it also necessary to include and briefly review the two neighbor's relationship; enforced by the special, long –term binding relations of the two neighbors throughout the ancient, medieval and present ages. They - Arabs and Europeans relationships - were sometimes characterized by conflict, sometimes by cooperation, exchange knowledge and culture; sometimes being occupied or sometimes the occupier. Fortunately, the current two relationships are now friendly and highly cooperative, especially after Europe discarded their old system of colonialism and super nationalism (for detail see Chapter 5).

In spite of the earlier failed total Arab market and unity attempts, many of the final declarations and recommendations of Arab Summits continue to recommend and call for Arab unity. This repeated approach, which is the realistic outstanding approach for the region's progress and advancement, was also used during the very recent Doha Summit (March 2009), wherein the heads of Arab countries recommended the long waited for: "a total Arab countries common, open free enterprise trade market"- first proposed way back in 1953. Other final Arab Summit declarations too called for many other forward Arab unity measures to be taken, including better coordination among the region's countries.

Presently, the Arab World is in a far superior position not only better than they were in the past but also much better than the economic status of many, for example, the Asia Pacific nations were when they decided to take the venture, the challenge and the transformation step from poor to prosperous economy (for more detail see Chapter 4). Again to emphasize, it is perfect time for the Arab region - governments and private sectors - to immediately perform the same smart act, with major benefits and great advantages to all: Arabs, Europeans and rest of the world as well!!

(How else can they- the Arab countries- revive their present economy and technology in presence of great wealth - capital and manpower - while continuing their earlier failed great Arab Common market, unity and progressive techno-economic plans? The act is being proposed here and by heads of Arab States during the Doha Summit; it should be certain and surely to be performed in presence of great regional wealth, readiness of EU and other advanced nations to aid in establishment and development of AU; avoiding the huge number of continuing and anticipated problems with soon doubling of future generation's population! Definitely the AU formation and development is beneficial to all regions' citizens: government or private sector. Regions' progressive, advance economy becomes the controlling and guiding principle and it shall overcome all *differences in the now economic: (rich and poor states), ideological (Sunnis versus Shiites or fundamentalist versus moderate forms of religion), Arab majority versus non-Arab minority and political (kingdom/sheikdom or republics) as well.* **If the Arab governments and population fail to take this golden opportunity, forming AU, then hell will be the only living place of the soon** *doubling Arab World population.* **"We planted for them and they ate; and we shall plant for them also to eat")**!

Finally as recommended throughout the book, in analogy to the first founding in 1957 of the six Western European nations of the EEC, followed then over the last 5 decades by gradually developing the union to its present European Union status, obligatory the Arabs can similarly and smartly, duplicate the act as proposed, by the six member GCC Arab Gulf union with the help and advice of the Arab League and "EU" aid as an advisor. Without a stressing harmful monetary finance, GCC can selectively complete the union, gradually expanding AU to include the rest of Arab nations. We are very much certain that AU sponsoring and endorsement by

GCC constitute a major stimulus to rush the rest of Arab countries to join the AU; no one dare to question this factual issue. This is discussed in further detail in "Conclusion Section" along with the above numerous benefits and superb advantages to Arab, European and other world's nations.

Introduction

Since the beginning of life on the planet earth, all living things: humans, animals and plants, required for their living and survival the three life-essentials: sun, air and water. It is no wondered that the first early primitive life developed in river valleys where both river water and warm weather were present. Life continues to depend on the three as natural sources of environmentally clean, renewable solar, wind and hydroelectric energy. They are needed in agriculture to produce human food as well as meet his many other environmental, industrial and other land requirements. The availability of the three in the various region of the planet, however, is seasonably climate variable, creating desert land in areas without water (such as in many parts of Arab world countries wherein ratio of desert to arable land is 87% to only 13%), rain forest in land with plenty of water and warm sun, frozen one where sun does not provide sufficient heat to keep it sufficiently warm (such as great parts of Russia and Canada are frozen land most of the year). In turn, the climate variation, regional and land physical structure, location in the planet induced drastic changes in quality and nature of the land, creating rich to moderately rich land, where the climate is great to a reasonably good one, to desolate unpopulated desert and frozen regions elsewhere.

The above natural earth and climate variation phenomena combined with the enormous, complex efforts in evolution of life on the planet, the ability of human to discover, develop and manage resources, including human ones, on national and regional efforts, resulted in division of the world into 'have'-developed- and 'have–not' –developing nations. Besides having a fertile land, necessary to support a sufficient number of populations to live on it; more than any other factor, this world divide, is attributed and dependent to a large extent, on the proper or lack of use of technology, economic plans. It is very much dependent and determined by the extent of nation's and human's efforts presently involved in other factors- R&D –based techno –economic and industrial developmental plans, simultaneously integrated with matching educational, technological, open free common market and industrial and social programs. R&D development and funding are quite important and critical and both are required to upgrade, maintain, innovate and improve nations' scientific, technological, economical and industrial development.

The worlds divide into developed and developing nations is a variable dynamic, liable to change case phenomenon. In the past we have seen, according to proven historical facts, that the Arabs declined in status from where they were during their Golden Age Era (750-1300) – united, having a huge market place, with a top status contributor to world science and knowledge- to their present developing status of 20 divided, none cooperative and none coordinating countries incapable of contribution to science nor knowledge neither to themselves nor to the world. On the other hand we have seen the European countries reverse the Arabs' trend by advancing its position from a war beaten, divided, exhausted imperial colonial region status, receiving US aid for 4 years- 1947-1951- to a presently fully integrated European Union of 31 European developed, rich nations having a huge open, free enterprise market (See Chapters 2, 3 and 5).

We also reported similar above fate achievement by: Japan- now second world richest economy in year 2006 to U.S.A; also a group of then emerging developing nations of East Asia Pacific Ridge countries of South Korea, Taiwan and Singapore plus others in Europe and elsewhere, who were able to gradually change their then developing nations status to that of a developed, advanced one in a few decades by following an advanced R&D-based techno-economic plan now used by all advanced and emerging world nations. Further advancements were also achieved even by the highly land extensive, highly populated word regions of China, Russia, Brazil and India by their adoption also of advanced nation's techno-economic plans. The astonishing accomplishment of many was achieved in spite of the many obstacles that confronted them during the status transformation process, including in many cases of severe poverty and military one single party rule (see Chapters 3 and 4).

These above various changes, which resulted in EU or other advanced or emerging nation's transformation to advanced status, further tell us that nations/regions could improve or drop their status by the nature and type of techno-economic and R&D plans they pursue in developing their status. The same concept led us too to initiate our present proposal: "how to change nations' techno-economic world order: from have-not, poor, underdeveloped to have, rich, develop nations' status". All advanced nations recognized and accepted the same; making R&D-based techno-economic development plans an integral inseparable and essential part of their entire short and long term planning's. They see that the plan is properly done, completely and regularly implemented and fully executed, otherwise it ends up in complete failure coupled with drop in nation/region's status. It became clear to them that continuing of status maintenance and improvement, requires following this fixed, dynamic, advance plan, putting special efforts, necessarily spending a good percentage of their GDP, about 3% with some nations spending more, on scientific, technological and innovative R&D works, which as well-known are essential and necessary tools for the maintenance and growth of their high tech industrial economy. R&D is also essential in order to protect, expand and improve trade balances in a highly competitive world market as well as ideal innovative means of discovering and identifying new rich products, businesses and markets.

Through the ages, utilizing the R&D process, the human race was able to introduce a great number of technological revolutions, many of which generated tremendous benefits to humanity. In most cases, they evolved from accidental and structured discoveries that were mostly based on the R&D processes, which were supported with ample capital investment, resulting in groundbreaking technological and economical innovations; the current great worldwide "Information Technology Revolution" being a classical example. Presently, there is great and sudden rush and emphasis, especially by advance nations, to search for an alternative energy sources, mainly renewable, environmentally friendly ones at consumers' affordable cost. The new R&D rush is being taken first to lower the now very expensive energy cost and second to counteract the environmental heat rise as a result of present world misuse of present energy systems. The great worldwide R&D emphasis and rush by many nations, governments and private enterprise companies to create innovative scientific or technological discoveries or to solve difficult problems are expected to add more funding to the great R&D expenditure in many very important fields of research and science.

The global spending on R&D already, which is spent mainly by the advanced nations, is expected to rise significantly to meet the demands of greatly expanding world population, allowing them to meet their numerous R&D essential techno-economical and other social requirements. Equally important elements to society advancement, besides good, favorable geopolitical and economical world conditions are: the countries' regional unity, common free enterprise market, regional security and peace, regional development and trade plans. **(Necessity is the mother of invention).**

Since the independence of many Arab countries from colonialism (1945-1980) and the establishment of the Arab League there were several movements to bring unity and advancement to the region's various countries, by the establishment of "a united Arab common market", which started way back in 1953. These unity and common market movements were encouraged then by many promoting, stimulus factors described later in Chapter 6, mainly same language (Arabic), same dominant religion (Islam), same culture and history heritage and having the Arab League. In spite of all these thought to be strong union promoting factors, favorable conditions, which were expected to quickly bring an all Arab common market and unity to the region; so far, for many, mainly then geopolitical and economical local and foreign reasons, these factors fail to deliver the Arab World countries the highly desired full Arab open common market or union (see Chapter 6, Section 6.3). One prime contributing factor to lack of achieving unity was the deeply rooted attachment and conviction of now and then past Arab leaders to the maintenance and preservation of self rule by the existing Arab governments. This conviction was exaggerated and extremely enhanced to guard against and prevent the many attempts to over through the existing Arab governments during the period 1950 to 1980.

Very much the same union promoting factors existed and were also common to the Spanish speaking people of South American Continent countries, wherein language (Spanish) and religion (Christian Catholicism) are, respectively, the official language and the dominant religion of the region. Additionally, all the 11 Spanish speaking countries are members of the "Union of South American Nations". (The 12th member is Brazil, a significantly large area and population country although resided by mostly Catholic followers, but their spoken language is Portuguese, kin to Spanish language). Again, similar to the failure of the above Arab World case, these assumed, would-be union promoting favorable, union and common open market stimulating conditions, so far also for many local and geopolitical and economical conditions plus others factors failed also to drive those Spanish countries, to achieve a union of free open market.

Evidently by themselves, these above considered and thought to be union stimulating factors were disappointedly insufficient to lead neither the Arab nor the Spanish countries regions' population to a regional common market and union formation nor it led them to the then anticipated developed status. On the other hand, in contradiction to the failure of Arab and Spanish speaking people of South American Continent regions and many others to form and implement regional unions, there were equally many high success union stories and major advances elsewhere in other parts of the world, where regional unity were achieved. The formation and gradual implementation over the last 5 decades of the "European Union" along with the adoption of an advanced R&D-based techno-economic plan on a grand scale is an example. Different promoting factors and conditions which were responsible for the failure are numerous and are beyond the scope of this book.

The EU formation and development exceeded all expectation and were by far one of the greatest told regional successful techno-economics' open regional common market and union stories. The "EU" was achieved in spite of the many differences in: official languages, Christian sects and European region's difference in development. It was achieved by use of proper sense, correct dialogue and discussion of union logic of great future benefits gained by an expanded open, free enterprise common market. Furthermore, the union was completed only by the ending of the immensely disastrous World War II, and European's recognition of the merits and value of a great expanded free enterprise open market.

Because EU's great success story it was selected as the appropriate regional model for an "Arab Union, which constitutes a primary candidate to benefit and subscribe to this proposed model [1, 2]. Under the super friendly relationship now existing between the two neighbors and the joint benefits gained by the two regions, the European Union and Arab regions, especially after Europe discarded colonialism; the EU stands to aid the Arab region catalyze a speedy formation and development of the proposed AU, again in the same way it catalyzed the European-Arab UM. The AU initiative is further encouraged especially when many of the Arabs region's authorities are now fully aware of the region's need for R&D-based technology to revive and vitalize the overall region's economy and world status [4, 5].

In spite of the above awareness and the tremendous wealth- capital and manpower so far accumulated in various parts of the region, for one reason and another, the region remained unable to form - "alone"- an all Arab common market or Arab union [6]. The many apparent problems standing in the way of previous total Arab unity attempts are summarized in Chapter 6, Section 6.3., though they are presently strongly confronted and encountered in the same chapter, Section 6.4, by a list of present equally abundant numerous factors and stimuli promoting and loudly screaming calling for an Arab common market governed by an Arab Union.

Modeling of AU on EU made it necessary to study the EU's procedural formation and development, combined furthermore with the witnessed great improvement of techno-economic status of the 31 EU members. Major advantages gained by the AU are numerous and are detailed under the "Summary Section". It further made it essential also to compare how the two neighbors- Europeans and the Arabs- faired with and without the union application. The various factors and means that lead to their present and past conditions are also briefly reviewed in the text (see Chapter 5).

Founding of an AU modeled on EU is beneficial not only to AU; definitely it is of great advantages to EU. It shall improve AU- EU's trade; investment and smooth flow of energy to it and world markets. Their AU and EU cooperation is expected to minimize if not to avoid massive migration of Arab nationals to Europe. All these facts reveal that the AU formation shall immensely help EU, in turn making it obligatory that EU aid AU's formation and development. The Arab world, now are at tech and economic disadvantage; they must seek EU's aid, cultivating the present great friendly relationship of the two regions. Improving EU and AU relations shall also allow the two regions better coordination, working together to avoid many future common problems and conflicts, solving their differences in an amicable, satisfactory way; the way EU now does its political and techno-economic relations with other advanced world's nations/ regions.

The proposal outlines the detailed necessary working steps and approach to be undertaken to successfully implement the "Arab Union Initiative", achieving its goal and realizing its objectives. As was done first by the 6 Western European Community in establishing first of the EEC market, gradually expanding, leading it eventually to the present EU formation; a select Arab states, preferably the 6 member GCC- based on its good achievement record as well as its fabulous richness- can initiate and start up the formation of a proposed "Arab Union" Common Market community, with the help and advice of the Arab League and "EU" aid as an advisor, catalyzing the AU formation process, gradually expanding AU to include the rest of Arab nations. Details of the proposed AU process formation and development with EU aid are fully described in Chapter 6.

"Oh long time sleepy Arab giant… wake-up, wake-up, wake-up, wake-up, you are now living in the 21st century and no longer in past eras! The way other advanced giant nations woke-up and achieved their technological and industrial advancement - even without the wealth of some Arabs now had/have - the Arab World can follow suit by developing their economy and technology through AU establishment; retrieving the glorious **Arab Golden Age** past **Era**; contributing to humanity, a deed nearly seize to exist over the past few centuries. Completion of your new Arab Union Initiative is extremely significant to the revival and awakening of Arab World; indeed constituting a modern Arab miracle. Your first realization and initial proposal for an open Arab open common market started way back in 1953. Call for it was repeated in almost most of the final Arab Summit declaration including the very recent Doha Summit (2009). **With present world financial and economic crisis, now the opportune time is to immediately start the implementation and no longer talk about AU anticipated formation;** particularly for the sake of the great poor Arab population, ratio 88%, and the present and future doubling generations as well.

At this point let us **pray for a future change** – after all the Arabs pray for every thing including always pray for rain. I pray to Al-mighty God to essentially awaken, guide and lead you - the Arabs – to unity, the way the Prophet Muhammad led most of you to accept Islam, the way Christ led some of you and most of Europe to accept Christianity, the way President Obama led them - the Americans - to accept him as a president and the way World Wars I & II led them-the European- to accept and form European Union)!!! Amine)

...   .

References

Jean Monnet/Robert Schuman Paper Series Vol.6 No.1 January 2006. "The European Union as a Model for Regional Integration: The Muslim World and Beyond,"

(see page about the author)
Arab League, Internet from Wikipedia, the free encyclopedia.
Kingdom to increase research and development spending to 2.5% of GDP, internet, 2006.

1. Sheikh Mohammed Al Maktoum launches foundation to promotehumandevelopment, www.forumblog.org/blog/2007/05/sheikh_mohammed.html

2. The United Nations Development Program (UNDP) released the Arab Human Development Report 2002, July 2, 2002. (The report, compiled by a "group of distinguished Arab intellectuals" led by Egyptian statistician Nader Fergany)

Chapter 1 – The Arab World

"This chapter was introduced to shed information, on Arab World region - the Cradle of Western Civilization and the region where the three monotheistic religions of Judaism, Christianity and Islam were started. Although they - the 3 religions - brought faith and believe in one god, they also are responsible for many of world conflicts and problems; hopefully they shall bring more coordination and understanding of these one same God faith. Because of great relevancy of the Arab region to the present proposal, especially AU formation and development modeled specifically on EU, the chapter was somewhat expanded. The information was further reviewed in some more detail in the Chapter 5 of the book. Specifically, all information compares the present (1945 to now) none cooperative, divided, fragment region into 20 separate countries to that of the region's union, open common market of the Golden Age Era (750-1300). During this earlier era the Arabs were masters of their destiny, able through the use of the 4 Islamic principles - Read, Write and perform R&D - to significantly contribute to advancement of world knowledge, science and literature. The formation of a proposed Arab Union modeled on European Unionon's formation shall also allow nowadays Arabs, through the use of the above 4 Islamic principles and modern techno-economic plans, not only to be awakened, considerably improve their techno-economic status but also to contribute to the advancement of their and world knowledg, science and literature as well".

To many in the West, the Arab World is the land of the tales of "One Thousand and One Arabian Nights and a Night", to the children it is the "land of tales: Sinbad the Sailor, Aladdin, Ali Baba and the Forty Thieves, the Flying Carpet, Magic Lamp, etc". To many others; it is the land of oil wealth, the very fancy, huge palaces of the many rich: kings, princes and sheiks that control both the oil and the land. Many others have the common misconceptions that the Arab World, the Middle East and the Islamic World are synonymous, the same one region. The truth, however, the three cover different regions of the world and can not be referred to as the Arab world. The Middle East or the Near East covers other parts of the East and only some parts of the Arab world; the North African part in particular is not included in the Middle East region. On the other hand, the Islamic world, which includes the Arab world, covers much larger group of 59 nations and larger part of the world area, especially in Asia, Africa, although

Muslims are found in sufficient number in parts of Europe and more recently in the Americas, where over 7 million American Muslims are in the United States alone.

The Arabian and "One Thousand and One Arabian Nights and a Night**" seen frequently on TV are from the Arabian fiction tales of the Arabic literature written during the Arab Golden Age (750- 1300) [1-4]. Also not all Arab land is oil rich, many of which does not have oil in their land and are not controlled by rich kings, princes and sheiks; the majority of the 20 Arab countries are republics [5]. Only 31% of Arab population is oil rich countries, the rest (69%) are not. (With the relatively large population of both Iraq and Algiers and the present war situation in Iraq, the ratio of rich to poor population is reduced now to 12: 88%).

Unlike the other misconception held by some people in the west that the Arab world is backward, they, the Arabs, have a highly-developed culture and civilization [1-4, 12-39, also see Chapter 5, Section 5.3], where modern cities are mixed with ancient ones from the time of the Roman Empire, Christ and the great Arab Caliphates and even many prior to these eras. In many aspects they are similar to many cities in the west and other great cities worldwide - some may be even more enchanting and charming, some others quite different from many western countries' cities in the world. During the Dark Ages in European history, the Arab-Islamic civilization was flourishing in the Middle East and North Africa. The Arab/Muslim state in southern Spain (Andalusia) was then the most advanced state in Europe [6]! During this time when Europe had lost most of the ancient masters' classical Roman and Greek knowledge, the Arabs were translating their philosophy texts into Arabic (750-1300) and preserved them to be rediscovered through the Arabic translations by the European during their awakening period (the Renaissance 1300-1600) [1-4]. They, the Arabs, then valued knowledge and for this purpose built great culture and civilization including schools, libraries and universities, which until now continued to be the world oldest continually functioning institutes, such as al-Azhar in Egypt (founded 975), Zaytouna in Tunisia, Al-Garaween in Morocco, etc [7].

Throughout the centuries, Arab World have made major contributions to the world religions, Arabic numbers and many other fields of sciences in mathematics, optics, medicine, history, philosophy, etc, [1-4, 12-19]. The Arabic numbers are used now worldwide. Arabic language and letters are used by many countries. The Arabic language was highly developed to the extant that there is no need for a second or third grade elementary school student now to use a dictionary for word spelling as is now the practice in English language.

History tell us also that the Arab countries - Mesopotamia the land of the two rivers and Egypt the land of the Nile - are the home of early ancient civilizations-"Cradle of Western

---

* "These are the tales that saved the life of Shahrazad; whose husband the king executed each of his wives after a single night of marriage. Beginning an enchanting story each evening, Shahrazad always withheld the ending to next night. The tales were told for a thousand and one nights later and her life was spared. Full of mischief, velour, ribaldry and romance, The Arabian Nights has enthralled readers for centuries"- Sir Richard Burton in his book on the same tales [39].

Civilization" [8] - established by the present Arab ancestors (ca 3500-500 B.C.). The region is also the place - the Holy Land, Iraq and Saudi Arabia - where the 3 monotheistic religions were started as well (1000 B.C. to 610 A.D.) with over 54% of whole world population followers of the three monotheistic religions [9]. Both – ancient civilization and religion - are major sources of tourist income to the region.

Contrary too, to the misconception by many people that all the Arab world land is dry and completely desert, a good portion of the land is not. The mountains of Lebanon and Syria, the Atlas mountains in North Africa - some of which are covered with snow - and other regions of the Mediterranean and northern Iraq as well as southern and some western parts of the Arabian Peninsula, southern Sudan receive sufficient rain to make it seasonally green, covered with vegetation. Together with many river valleys that are lush and green, they produce large quantities of products, cereals, cotton, fruits and vegetables and other crops for the region. The Tigris and Euphrates in Iraq and Syria, the Nile in Egypt and Sudan, the Orontes in Syria, the Jordan river and others rivers in North Africa are among the Arab world's major rivers. A great portion of this fertile land is planted, some with more than one crop per year.

Despite the presence of rivers and the many bodies of water in the region, the Arab world continues to be among the poorest nations of the world in natural water resources, facing a critical water shortage and as a result food production shortage. In some parts of the Arab region, the severe water shortage is partially covered with fresh water extracted from the sea by the desalination process. Presently, the Arabian region, in particular the Gulf region, leads the world in seawater desalination industry, producing over 60% of desalinated seawater worldwide. With the tremendous increases expected in the region' population, now, water is more precious than oil. This severe water shortage problem combined with food production shortage came as a result of lack of water. Water is used also to support the populations and industries, now constitutes the main critical problem facing the Arab's region. Besides the Gulf region, other Arab regions need seawater desalination but most of them so far can not afford it. The water shortage and other shortages problems, entirely dependent on the availability of the life essential substance water, can find their solution in producing fresh water from seawater in abundance at affordable cost through the development of seawater desalination process technology [10].

The present, modern Arab world land extends from the Atlantic Ocean in the west to the Indian Ocean in the east, a distance of over (5000 miles or about 8000 km), and from the Mediterranean Sea in the north to Central Africa in the south. By all measures, the region covers a huge land area of over 12.9 million square kilometer (over 5 million square miles). The Arab World total area is the size of the entire Spanish-speaking Western Hemisphere of South American continent, also of 12.9 million square kilometers, larger than Europe including European part of Russia (10.4 million), Canada (10 million), China (9.6 million), the United States (9.6 million), Brazil (8.7 million). Only Russia – at seventeen million square kilometers, the largest country in the world – and the combination of Canada and USA in North America, as one cultural unit (20 million square kilometers) are larger in area [11].

The Arab World consists of 20 neighboring, adjacent countries within two continents: Algeria, Egypt, Mauritania, Morocco, Sudan, Tunisia and Western Sahara (administered by Morocco) all are in Africa, while Bahrain, Iraq, Jordan, Kuwait, Lebanon, Libya, Palestine, Qatar, Saudi Arabia, Syria, United Arab Emirates and Yemen, all are in Asia (see map Figure 1). The combined Arab countries population is presently – year 2008 - about 329 million people (see Table 1) and are expected to reach double this number by the upcoming two decades. Larges population of over 80 millions is Egypt while the lowest one is Bahrain; population is less than710, 000 persons. Table 1 also shows total GDP for the region and that per each Arab country, wherein the oil producing Kingdom of Saudi Arabia GDP is over $481 billion to less than $3.2 billion for Mauritania. The Arab's GDP issue is discussed in further detail in Chapter 2.

The central location of the Arab World countries shared between two continents at the edge of western Asia: Europe to the north and west, and Asia: language, culture, civilization, religions, race mix, science, knowledge and history. This central position of the region was equally a detrimental factor in the transformation, formation, rule and present

Figure 1 – Map of Arab World Countries

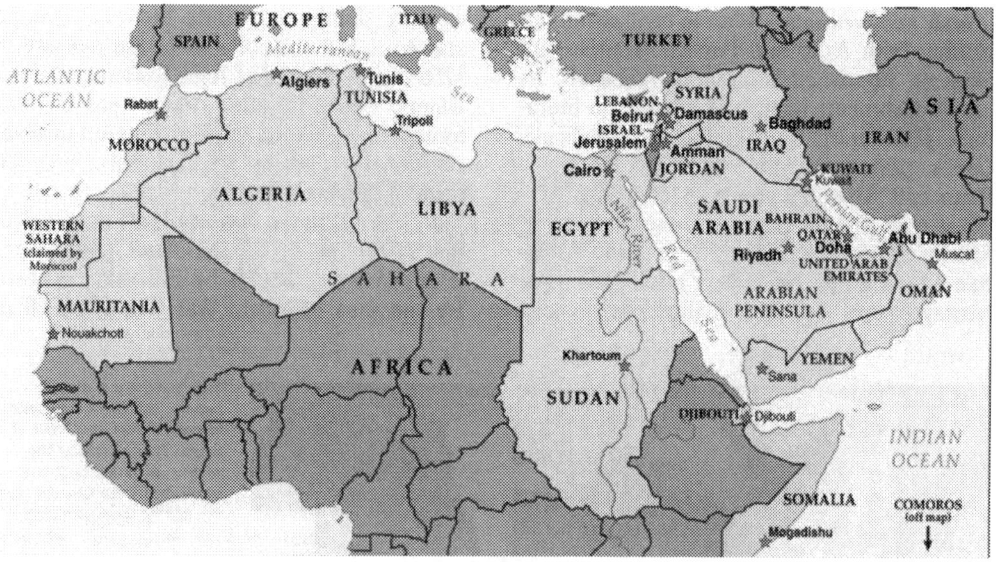

Table 1 – Arab Countries Population and GDP – 2008 (source CIA World Fact book 2008)

Country	Population	GDP (USD million)
Egypt	80,335,036	162,164
Sudan	39,379,358	57,911
Morocco	33,757,175	86,394
Algeria	33,333,216	159,669
Saudi Arabia	27,601,038	481,631
Iraq	27,499,638	90,907
Yemen	22,230,531	27,151
Syria	19,314,747	54,803
Tunisia	10,276,158	40,348
Jordan	6,053,193	20,030
Libya	6,036,914	100,071
UAE	4,444,011	260,141
Lebanon	3,925,502	28,939
Mauritania	3,270,065	3,161
Oman	3,204,897	52,584
Palestine	4,018,332	6,641
Kuwait	2,505,559	158,089
Qatar	907,229	102,302
Bahrain	708,573	21,236
Total	**328,801,172**	**1,914,172**

Table 2– Arab World by Region

Region			Population	GDP (USD million)
Gulf Cooperation Council (GCC)			39,370,307	1,075,983
United Arab Maghreb (UAM)			86,608,356	389,643
Arab Mediterranean Union*			221,001,852	662,220
Oil Rich Countries			106,240,071	1,426,630
Total (Arab World)			328,801,172	1,914,172

*Includes UAM

neighbors. It played a major role in determining the development, division and shaping of the Arab world as well as those of the neighboring countries' within their the old world regions; in particular the Mediterranean, Europe regions, parts of Africa and countries of western Asia.

More precisely, the formation and make up of modern Arab world countries has its origin in the medieval ages during the introduction of the third monotheistic Islamic religion (610-

632 A.D.) by the Prophet Muhammad (570-632 A.D.) in what is now western Saudi Arabia [1-4]. With an astonishing speed, the Arab territories were extended within 117 years from the Arabian Peninsula - the Arab origin - to rule, control and cover all the land between Spain (including Spain itself) in the west to the borders of China in the east [1-4, 12,19]. The first expansion was during the rule of the first Al-Rashidoun Caliphates (633-656), capital Al-Medina, Saudi Arabia, followed second by the Arab Empire Umayyad dynasty Caliphates, capital Damascus, Syria (661-750 A.D.). Unlike the Umayyad the rule of the third Caliphates Abbasids dynasty (750-1258 A.D.) from their newly built capital, Bagdad, did not engage in further major expansion of an already huge Caliphates empire's land [1-4, 12]. They concentrated their efforts on actively developing the society by the development of commerce and trade, arts, manufacturing, the government system, the overall culture and nation's civilization. Development and encouragement of science, know how and technology flourished during this Arab Golden Age Era (750-1300) [1-4, 12-18, 19-30]. Our discussion will be limited to the progress and market development during the present and the Arab Golden Age Era.

The enlightened early Abbasids dynasty Caliphates actively directed the society to seek knowledge using the four Islamic principles **(Reading, Writing and perform R&D)** and scholarship by learning science, architect and philosophy developed by others and at the same time contributing their own development of the same. Their trade covered an open free market within the empire, neighboring parts of Africa; in addition of maintaining a shipping and land-trade routes with several foreign trading parties. Their international trade extended eastward up to India, China and beyond and westward to cover the Mediterranean countries and parts of Europe [1- 4, 12]. The expanded trade is credited by spreading Islam in Southern India, Bangladesh, Malaysia, South Philippine and Indonesia, now the most populated Islamic country in the world. This era reached its **"Golden Age of Arab/Moslem civilization"** during the rule of the Great Haroun Al Rashid and three sons (796-842) [14]. With the great development of knowledge within the region Golden Age, Arabic became the language of: communication, learning, science, literature including fiction as already mentioned [1-4, 12].

The collapse of the Abbasids Caliphates' by the Mongol invasion which destructed Bagdad in the year 1258 [15] and shrinkage of their rule to parts of the empire a variety of Arab and Moslem Sultanate and Kingdoms ruled the various regions of the empire(950-1800). It is during this period -of the Caliphate and the following period of the Sultanate and Kingdoms (632-1800) - more than any other period during the long history of the region - that gave birth and the making of what is known now as the modern Arab World [1-4]. This period was further responsible for making Arabic and Islam the language and religion of the region and the many other dominating aspects of its present culture. Although Islam became the dominant religion of the present Arab World population, there are sizable numbers of Christians, living primarily in Lebanon, Egypt, Palestine, Iraq, Jordan, Sudan and Syria. There were also a significant minority of Arab Jews living throughout the Arab World; however, most of them immigrated to Israel, with only a small segment remained.

By the end of the rule of various Sultans and Kings that followed the Abbasids rule, during the early part of the 19th and 20th centuries, a large part of the Arab countries were controlled and ruled by the new imperial European kingdoms and empires. The imperial European powers kept the region's culture, as it was, without interfering in changing the region's language nor religion, although they tried to teach some of the population their own language and culture. By the end of World War II (1945) or short time thereafter, the Arab world countries got their independence, unfortunately winding up divided, mostly by the help and in certain cases the decision of the then controlling colonial powers, into a pseudo division that constituted the present division of the present 20 modern Arab countries(see Fig. 1). The observed border straight lines in the Arab World map, artificially drawn by these European colonial powers during this imperialism period, came as a result of this pseudo partition.

A large segment of the region's population who now lives in Arab World is not necessarily of 100% Arab origin. With establishment of the great Arab empire and spreading of Islam during the seventh and eighth centuries as well as later on, there was a great natural homogenization and assimilation process of the Arabs - through marriage with the region's indigenous population or through large migration of Arabs from the Arabian Peninsula. This process extended nearly over the past 14 centuries. As a result of this assimilation process and the dominant use of Arabic language and Islam by the population, the whole region's citizens, all now identify themselves as Arabs, with the exception of a small ratio of minority groups such as: Berber in North Africa, the nomadic Touareg people (also of Berber origin) in the Sahara desert, Kurds in the northern regions of Iraq (15-20%) and Syria (5-10%). This is the equivalent to what happened, for example in USA, where each citizen regardless of his ancestor origin now identifies himself as an American.

Although they joined the Arab League in 1974, the Somalia's and Djibouti are non-Arab countries, with only some small mixed and ethnic Arab groups. Arabic, however, is the second official language of Somalia and is one of the official languages in Djibouti.

Different forms of government are now represented in the Arab World: Some of the countries are traditional monarchies or sheikdoms: Bahrain, Jordan, Kuwait, Morocco, Oman, Qatar, Saudi Arabia and the United Arab Emirates. The remaining Arab countries are republics, but in all cases the rule tends to be inherited, sometime, and unfortunately dictatorial in nature.

Although the region is actively engaged in introducing universal education for both sexes, nevertheless more than one third of youth remained illiterate in some of the Arab World and Arab League Countries [31].According to UNESCO, the average rate of adult literacy in the Arab region among the youth (ages 15-24) of 63.9 in year1990 increased to 76.3 % in year 2002. By comparison, the average rate of GCC States however was 94 %, followed by the western (Maghreb) Arabs at 83.2%. There exist over 100 universities in the region, where over 40% of their yearly graduates are exported, many to advanced countries!

The wealth of Arab countries consists of:

- Their huge, extensive land (of over 12.9 million square kilometer of about 5 million square miles).

- The sea, where the Arab lands itself is bordered with two oceans: the Atlantic in the west, and the Indian in the east plus three large seas: the Mediterranean, the Red and Gulf seas, for a total of about 23,000 km.

- Manpower and consumers, with a combined population of over 329 million people is expected to reach double this number by the year 2025 or thereabout.

- Let's not forget one extremely important wealth source, the natural resources, mainly oil and gas reserves; also other minerals such as iron, copper, phosphate, potash, and many others.

- Agriculture and products constitute another large source of income to the region.

- Although present region's industrial contribution continue to be insufficient to raise the region's income to the level of advanced nations status, nevertheless, the region possesses the means for potentially great future industrialization: vast wealth of raw materials, large manpower including potentially skilled thousands yearly graduates from more than 100 universities and other technical schools spread all over the region; all strongly supported by the proposed AU formation.

- Tourism and religious pilgrimage- the Arab World is the place also contribute to the wealth of the region. The place is where the Cradle of Western Civilization and the region where the three monotheistic religions of Judaism, Christianity and Islam were started.

Agriculture is the primary economic activity in most of the Arab homeland. The most important food crops produced in the region are wheat, barley, rice, maize, dates and millet. Fruits and vegetables are grown in large quantities, satisfying the region' need, some shipment of fruits and vegetables are exported, mainly to Europe. Cash crops, grown in large quantities within the region are sugarcane and sugar beets which are exported (as sugar) along with cotton and sesame seeds.

Some Arab countries have substantial reserves of petroleum and associated gas reserves, providing great wealth to the region. The combined total of seven Arab states account for about 50.55% of world total oil reserve: Saudi Arabia 21.22%, the largest in world oil reserve as well as largest producer of it, Iraq 8.87%, Kuwait (7.83%), the UAE (7.56%), Libya 3.02%, Qatar 1,17% and Algeria 0.88%[5]. Oman is also an oil exporter. Other Arab countries: Bahrain, Yemen, Egypt, Sudan, Syria, Morocco (Western Sahara), all have smaller but significant reserves satisfying demand of local market and many maintain oil export, although limited.

Where the oil reserves are present, they have significant effects on regional wealth and politics, standard of living, leading to economic disparities between oil-rich and oil-poor Arab countries. The sparingly populated oil rich states of the Gulf and Libya (their total population about 12% of total Arab population) have the greatest wealth, triggering extensive labor immigration to these parts of the Arab World. However, the majority of Arab countries, although many have large oil reserves and large population, such as Iraq and Algiers, do not presently have such large per capita wealth (see Chapter 2).

Many of the Arab countries have also substantial reserves of natural gas, especially Algiers and Qatar and recently Egypt also has sizable reserves. All the three are gas exporters. Associated gas, which flows with oil in oil producing countries, is produced in many cases in sufficient quantities, satisfying the local market need. Other Arab countries have sizable reserve of phosphate, iron, sand shale, uranium and other minerals.

Saudi Arabia remains the top Arab economy in terms of total GDP (ranked 25th among richest nations) became more so by the very large expansion of price of oil. It is one of Asia's largest economies (ranked 6th in Asia), followed by Algeria and Egypt, which were also in 2006 the second and third largest economies in Africa (after South Africa). Other Gulf oil producing countries have high per capita income (see Chapter2) but they have very low population, some less than 700,000 while the rest less than 3 millions.

Besides lack of total Arab union, uniting the Arabs and their collective common approach in solving the numerous problems confronting the region, the highly utterly divided region is now suffering from these problems and is not seriously searching for a common collective techno-economic solution. These problems and a proposal for the solution by: the establishment and development of an Arab Union modeled on European Union; lifting of the region's techno-economic case from developing to develop status, are described in the following sections of the book.

...   .

References

1. Philip K. Hitti, The History of the Arabs, New York, Palogrove McMillan, 2002, 10th Edition, 822 pages, first edition published 1937.

2. Albert Hourani, Arab History, Oxford Press, December 2003.

3. The Oxford History of Islam, Editor John L. Esposito, Oxford University press, 749 pages, with 15 contributors.

4. Patricia S. Daniel and Stephen G. Hyslop, Almanac of World History, Library of Congress Publication, 2003.

5. U.S. Energy Information, Greatest Oil Reserve, Oil & Gas Journal, Vol.105, No.4, Dec. 2005.

6. Cordoba, Spain, from Wikipedia, the Free Encyclopedia.

7. for example, AL-Azher, Wikipedia, the Free Encyclopedia.

8. Cradle of Western Civilization, Patricia S. Daniel and Stephen G. Hyslop, Almanac of World History, Library of Congress Publication, 2003 (page 460).

9. Major Religion of the World, Ranked by size and number of Adherents, www.google.com/search.

10. Ata M. Hassan, a Blue Revolution, San Diego, CA, U.S., 2006.

11. Arab World, Wikipedia, the Free Encyclopedia.

12. Apostasy War, pages 11-12, The Oxford History of Islam, Editor John L. Esposito, Oxford University press, 749 pages, with 15 contributors.

13. ibid, pages 12, 312, Al-Yarmuk Battle.

14. ibid, pages 27, 32 plus others under Harun Al-Rashid.

15. ibid, pages 59, 695, Mongols sack Bagdad, also see [1-4].

16. ibid, pages 37, 60, Fatimid's Caliphs.

17. ibid, pages 327,339, Saladin as crusader's opponent, see also [1-4].

18. ibid, pages 365, 422, Ottoman Empire.

19. Mesopotamia Civilization, 3500-500 B.C., Pages 40-50, **Patricia S. Daniel and Stephen G. Hyslop, Almanac of World** History, Library of Congress Publication, 2003.

20. ibid, pages 50-55, Egyptian Civilization, 3000-500 B.C.

21. ibid, pages 62-65, Mediterranean Civilization, 3000-500 B.C.

22. ibid, pages 94-95, Alexander the Great, 336-323 B.C.

23. ibid, page 49, The Patriarch Abraham of Ur introduces Judaism.

24. ibid, pages 56-59, Indian Civilization, 2500-500 B.C.

25. ibid, pages 60-61 Chinese Civilization, 2200-500 B.C.

26. ibid, pages 80-85, the Roman Civilization and Empire, 509 B.C.-476 A.D.

27. ibid, pages 110-113, The Byzantine Empire and   Civilization, B.C.

28. ibid, pages 72-73, The Persian Empire and Civilization, 550 B.C.- 651 A.D.

29. ibid, pages 98-99, Christ introduce Christianity, 27 A.D.

30. ibid, page 99, Christianity declared religion of the Byzantine Empire, 390 A.D.

31. UNESCO Report on education in the Arab World, 2004.

32. Source: Opening speech of Mahmoud Khoudri, Algeria's Industry Minister, at the 37th General Assembly of the Iron & Steel Arab Union, Algiers, May 2006.

33. The formation of the Arab League, Wikipedia, the Free Encyclopedia.

34. UAR Formation, Wikipedia, the Free Encyclopedia.

35. GCC Formation, Wikipedia, the Free Encyclopedia.

36. UM Formation, Wikipedia, the Free Encyclopedia.

37. *Nature* **444**, 35-36 (2 November 2006): 10.1038/444035, Islam and science: Where are the new patrons of science?

38. Arabic text of Arab League Summit Meeting Recommendation, Doha, Qatar, March 2009.

39. Sir Richard Burton, The Arabian Nights, The Book of a Thousand Nights and One Night, CRW Publishing Limited, 2007.

Chapter 2 - the World's Have and Have-Not Nations

The world as already stated is divided into fortunate have (developed, rich) and unfortunate have-not (developing, relatively poor) nations. In general, the have nations live in what is known as the nations of the North: Europe, U.S.A, Canada, Australia, Brazil; also some nations live in parts of Asia (Japan, Asia Pacific Ridge countries, South Korea, Taiwan, Singapore, Hong Kong, China), while the have-not occupy the rest of the world - known otherwise as the people of the South - in Asia, Africa and Latin America, with some pockets of have population found among them. Contrary to the poor nations, which so far kept away from application of modern up-to-date economical planning, the rich nations rigidly, routinely applied them in their economic planning.

Table 1 shows the 20 richest (Table 1a) and 5 poorest (Table 1b), nations of the world ranked according to the country's national annual GDP income for the year 2004-2008, while Table 2 shows the 20 leading (Table 2a), and 5 least GDP per capita (Table 2b) world nations for the years2004- 2007 [1]. By far, the 5 richest nations are: United States, Japan, Germany, China, and United Kingdom with an International Monetary Fund estimated total GDP - Purchasing Power Parity (PPP) - national income per 2008 annum of each: $14,195, $4,818, $3,653, $3,942, and$2,833 billion U.S. Dollars, respectively, as compared to less than $370 million U.S. Dollars per 2008 annum for each of the bottom ranked last 5 countries. Notice the great difference in GDP annual income for some nations between the years 2004-2008, wherein for example China, Brazil, Russia and Turkey GDP's the income more than doubled compared to a nearly stagnant GDP for Japan, narrowly

Table 1a – GDP ($ billion) for Top 20 Nations

Rank	Country	2004	2005	2006	2007	2008
	United States	11,686	12,434	13,195	13,844	14,195*
	Japan	4,608	4,561	4,377	4,384	4,867*
	Germany	2,749	2,796	2,916	3,322	3,653*
	China	1,932	2,244	2,645	3,251*	3,942*
	UK	2,169	2,246	2,402	2,773	2,833*
	France	2,061	2,137	2,252	2,560	2,843*
	Italy	1,730	1,779	1,858	2,105	2,330*
	Spain	1,046	1,132	1,232	1,439	1,623*
	Canada	994	1,135	1,275	1,432	1,571*
	Brazil	664	882	1,072	1,314	1,621*
	Russia	592	764	989	1,290	1,699*
	India	669	783	877	1,099	1,233*
	S. Korea	681	792	888	957*	999*
	Australia	641	713	756	909	1,047*
	Mexico	683	768	840	893	950*
	Netherlands	611	634	671	769*	863*
	Turkey	393	483	529	663	748*
	Sweden	358	367	394	455	503*
	Belgium	359	376	398	454	507*
	Indonesia	257	286	364	433*	488*

* Estimates

Table 1b – GDP ($ billion) for Bottom 5 Nations

Rank	Country	2004	2005	2006	2007	2008
177	Guinea-Bissau	0.27*	0.302*	0.308*	0.343*	0.368*
178	Dominica	0.272	0.284	0.301	0.311*	0.327*
179	Tonga	0.182	0.215	0.223	0.219*	0.224*
180	São Tomé	0.108	0.114	0.123*	0.144*	0.157*
181	Kiribati	0.059	0.063	0.063*	0.067*	0.071*

* Estimates

escaping a   decline in 2008 GDP as compared to that of 2004 GDP. All other countries show a rise in income with Canada GDP income rising by 58% and India nearly doubled. (What a great difference in GDP annual income between the have and the have-not nations).

On the other hand, the 5 leading GDP per capita countries are: Qatar, Luxemburg, Norway, Brunei and Singapore with 2007 estimated annual GDP per capita for each of: $80,870, $80,457, $53,037, $51,005 and $49,714 U.S. dollars, respectively, (or earning of $221- $136 per capita per day) as compared to only less than $485 U.S. dollars per annum (range $484 -$188) for the 5 bottom ranked all African countries. Again, notice what a great difference in GDP per capita income between the have and the have-not nations, wherein the **yearly** annual per capita income of the 5 African countries in bottom of the list ranged between $484 -$188 is not much greater than that of **daily** earning of a high GPD per capita income of 5 richest nations of $221- $136.

Notice, also that all the countries within the 5 highest GDP per capita in Table2, are not the same countries as the 5 richest world countries shown in Table1. In Table 2, only 2 countries are European countries, meanwhile 3 are Asiatic countries, two of which are oil-rich exporting countries. The GDP per capita for the 2 European countries are largely inflated by the large recent Euro- U.S. dollar currency conversion rates (see Figure 1) [2].

Unlike the have-not nations, which tend to have an agrarian none advanced and none developed economy, largely dependent on agriculture for their living, characterized by their very low to minimum of R&D activity; by contrast, the rich nations, as shown later, utilize modern, developed techno-economic means and plans in running their industrial economy, spending a good percentage of their annual GDP, in some cases up to 5%, on Research and Development activity to upgrade, maintain and innovate their scientific and techno-economic states, to continue maintaining their world leadership wealth- and trade-wise.

It gives many humans worldwide severe pain and great anger, as it did to us, discovering such large differences in income between the very rich and the very poor nations of our world. With such very low income, especially for the poorest nations, wherein during the year 2007, the GDP income per capita for the lowest ranked 7, nations out of total 181 nations of our world amounts to less than $484[1] per same year 2007.

Table 2a – GDP per Capita (PPP) for Top 20 Nations

Rank	Country	2004	2005	2006	2007
	Qatar	68,166	70,772	76,537	80,870*
	Luxembourg	65,668	69,984	75,395	80,457*
	Norway	45,154	47,786	50,203	53,037*
	Brunei	47,377	47,465	50,472	51,005*
	Singapore	39,994	43,333	46,863	49,714*
	U. S.	39,812	41,970	44,118	45,845
	Ireland	36,089	38,226	40,669	43,144*
	Hong Kong	32,298	35,550	38,838	41,994*
	Switzerland	34,856	36,608	38,919	41,128*
	Kuwait	35,978	36,953	38,072*	39,306*
	Iceland	32,592	35,256	37,019	38,751
	Netherlands	33,122	34,736	36,833	38,486*
	Canada	33,353	35,111	36,837	38,435
	Austria	32,737	34,107	36,215	38,399*
	Denmark	31,764	33,593	35,896	37,392*
	U. A. E.	30,954	32,751	35,882	37,293*
	Sweden	30,942	32,706	34,865	36,494*
	Australia	31,551	32,898	34,375	36,258*
	Finland	29,227	30,496	32,859	35,280*
	Belgium	30,559	31,963	33,694	35,273

*Estimates

Table 2b – GDP per Capita (PPP) for Bottom 5 Nations

Rank	Country	2004	2005	2006	2007
176	Guinea-Bissau	448*	464*	473*	484*
177	Burundi	329*	335*	356*	372*
178	Liberia	306	312	333	357
179	Congo	256*	276*	291*	309*
180	Zimbabwe	203*	200*	195*	188*

*Estimates

Such highly populated countries as India and China, with population of each of over one billion person, have 2007 GDP per

Figure 1 – Euro to Dollar Exchange Rate 2000-2005

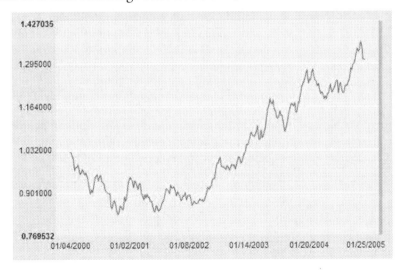

capita income per annum of only $1056 and $3305, respectively. Many other highly populated nations GDP per capita per annum income falls within this category, making the majority of world population having such low income of less than $3,305 per person per 2007 annum.

In spite of the very much greater buying power of the dollar in poor countries than those in rich countries, still the difference in their respective income is vastly great! This great difference in GDP per capita per annum income between the have and have-not raises the question: "how these poor nations, particularly nations with per capita income of less than $1,000 per annum, can afford to manage, to take care of their poor, struggling population: keep them well-fed, well-educated, protect them from hunger, disease, etc,?" It is the obligation and is a must, for the well-to-do rich, industrial nations to provide the necessary help and financial and technical aid to revive and improve the overall living standards and techno-economic conditions of these poor, unfortunate, under privileged countries and peoples with benefits to all. The prevailing conditions as shown in Reference [1] indicate the very insufficiency of the present rich nations' aid to the poor people of our world.

The sad situation of great inequality in income between the have and have-not nations, especially in low per capita income nations, alarmed the U.N to act on this issue. During the Millennium Summit(September 2000), attended by 189 government leaders from the highest political level of almost every country in the world, the UN launched and agreed on to a set of eight time-bound targets that, when achieved, will end extreme poverty across the planet [3]! Two years later, in October 2002, the United Nations' campaign informed, inspired and encouraged people's involvement and action for the realization of the Millennium Development Goals (MDG) to assist the poorer nations to eradicate poverty and world hunger, with water as the key to the success and accomplishment of each of the 18 goals of this U.N ambitious MDG plan [4].

Placing water "as the key to the success and accomplishment of U.N ambitious MDG plan" was correctly chosen since the witnessed poverty in many poor nations, of the world has its root in their water poverty, quantity and quality-wise. The essence of life – water – without it, Earth would be a moon-like desert, void of life. Water is not only very essential to drink and satisfy other domestic uses but equally essential in agriculture for food production as well as for industrial work and development; it is necessary for improvement and creation of healthy environment, high quality none polluted water is essential to avoid diseases including deadly ones plus it is required for many other human, animal and plant needs. The Blue Revolution (BLRV) is being introduced by the author [5], in affirmation of: the U.N Millennium Development Goals, the Green Revolution plus other charitable organizations to eradicate and overcome many of the extreme poverty and hunger problems of poor world nations. The BLRV goals are to: develop seawater desalination processes, allowing extracting fresh water from the sea in abundance at an affordable cost, at its international R&D institutes, availing the technology, free of charge, to all who needs it. The BLRV is also in affirmation of President Clinton's Global Initiative, founded September 2005 by President Clinton [6]. All these initiatives plus many others, such as the new Africa's Green Revolution [7], were introduced to fight world Poverty. We strongly believe that all activities can help the poor nations climb out of their poverty, misfortune, and misery.

Working at both the <u>national</u> and international levels, the ambition of the MDG Campaign is to inspire a global movement to achieve the Goals and eradicate extreme poverty by 2015. The importance of the subject by working on MDG Campaign led to the creation of a special secretariat, housed at UNDP headquarters in New York. Furthermore, the U.N. considered the premise to be simple in that "**we are the first generation that can put an end to extreme**

poverty around the world, and we refuse to miss this opportunity"! How about that greatly said statement but how effectively it was done?

In cooperation with U.N. at the G8 Summit in Gleneagles, Scotland 2005, they focused on Africa and climate change. They agreed to double aid to Africa and to eliminate outstanding debts of the poorest countries, not only in Africa but worldwide. As outlined in the Gleneagles communiqué the G8 nations will together increase aid to developing countries by around $50 billion by year 2010. Of this, at least $25 billion will go to poor nations in Africa. The G8 leaders also promised increased support for African peacekeeping forces to help to deter, prevent and resolve conflicts in Africa, and pledged additional investment in education and the fight against HIV/AIDS, malaria, tuberculosis and other killer diseases [8].

Definitely, The G8 has the capability and skill to fund and to meet the MDG Campaign. Without any financial or technical burden, they have the capital to fund the MDG Campaign and the skilled manpower and industrial capability to provide the necessary aid to solve many of the problems confronting the world's poor. Together, the West, East Asia and other world rich nations West, East Asia and other world rich nations, the U.N., the World Bank numerous world charitable organizations, other world communities and other governments in Europe and the oil-rich nations; all can contribute significantly to the completion and realization of this essential, humane program to bring it, at least to a significant partial reality and solution.

How the above promises and assumptions were realized? The promised aid to poor nations by the G8 did not fully materialized. Two years later, at Heiligendamm, Germany, summit, June 2007[9], the G8 leaders did not acknowledge their failure to deliver. In fact, the G8's performance has actually deteriorated. Comparing Official Development Assistance (ODA) figures between 2005 and 2006, in percentage of national income, "the U.S. fell from 0.22 to 0.17, Italy from 0.29 to 0.20 and Japan from 0.28 to 0.25, while France and Germany stagnated at 0.47 and 0.36 respectively; only the U.K., because of special relations, increased from 0.47 to 0.52". In order to make things worst, "a large share of aid delivered in the past two years has actually been debt relief (much of that for Iraq)". Thus, these actual facts represent a regression rather than progress of the Gleneagles G8 summit commitments.

The picture for sub-Saharan Africa is bleak; excluding debt relief, aid to the region is stagnant, and no poor country has seen the increase in aid that would enable the region to achieve the Millennium Development Goals by the year 2015. This case occurred, although the G8 announced in their Heiligendamm 2007 summit, the sum of $60 billion to fight HIV/AIDS, malaria, and tuberculosis, but much of this money was previously pledged and lacked timelines for delivery.

Now, with the financial and economic crisis presently confronted the world, the advanced nations rose to the occasion, such as U.S.A., EU, Japan, China coordinating with G8 and G7 and the 20 wealthiest nations during their Summit, pledging cooperation and huge bailout sum of capital to confront the financial and economic crisis. The very recent 20 nations Summit in London, April 2009, they pledged $1.1 Trillion global bailout to revive world trade and economy as well as help developing countries encounter the present world financial and economic crisis. The recent (July 2009) G8 Summit meeting in Italy, held with some representatives of developing and emerging nations, pledged additional $20 billions to assist poor countries. Again, how effective the promised aid to the many developing nations remains to be seen!

What the poor countries in Africa and rest of the world need now, in addition to have the funds and aid to enable them to meet the MDG, to feed their population, compact deadly diseases, improve agriculture, development of water resources and very important to improve education, is gaining the necessary technology and know how, to develop industry as already proposed here for the Arab World and other less developed nations (see Chapter 6). So far, the aid to African Sub-Sahara region was mainly in compacting deadly HIV/AIDS, malaria, and tuberculosis diseases, partially fighting hunger and thirst and very little in development and industrialization. World aid by the rich's emphasis continues on how to keep the poor population surviving, in testimony to their inability to extend effective help measures to aid the world poor overcome their many distressing problems. Their main concern (the rich) is some thing else: is in how to get richer, continuing to ignore their obligation and commitment to effectively help the world poor! The outcome of this neglect is harmful to all, rich and poor. This is why we see many demonstrations, riots and some uprising in London, Washington and many other places worldwide in support of rich , advanced nations aid and help the poor nations overcome their poverty and misery; a legitimate, honorable and humane cause.

There is numerous other have-not countries in the world which need rich countries' aid, they, however, tend to maintain better overall conditions than the poorest countries in Africa. It is beyond the scope of this investigation to study all of them. One case, which is the subject of this study - the Arab World' case - have and have-not situation, deserves to be briefly discussed along with have oil-rich Arab countries.

2.1 Arab World Have- oil-rich- and Have-not Countries

Table 3 lists the per capita income of Arab countries for the year 2004-2008 [1], while Table 3a lists the same per region along with its population. The GDP per capita income, year 2008, for the rich GCC Arab countries varies from as high as $84,833 to $24,240 for oil-rich exporter Qatar and Saudi Arabia, respectively. (Total GCC's population is only about 39 millions compared to about 329 million for Arab World total, Table 1, Chapter1). These figures compare to the very low ones of: $2,123 for Mauritania, with Iraq, Yemen and Sudan did not fair much better, see Table3, each with GDP income per capita of: $3,600, $2,406 and $2,322, respectively, and to only $1,100 GDP per capita/annum, year 2007, for Palestinians in both West Bank and Gaza!!

Indeed, a very huge difference is seen between the two GDP incomes per capita of the GCC's rich and the rest of poor Arab countries (Table 3a). Other high GDP per capita income for the year 2008 is shown in same Table 3, with other major oil-producing and exporting countries per capita (PPP)/annum income of: Qatar, Kuwait, United Arab Republic, Oman and of course Saudi Arabia, which is the undisputed world leader in oil- production and exporter of this presently very expensive product, were: $84,833, $40,873, $38,107, $26,022 and $24,240, respectively.

The GDP per capita income in year 2008 of other Arab major oil- producing and exporting countries: Libya, Algeria of $13,361 and $7,939, respectively, are far less than that of the above 5 Gulf Arab countries. The GDP per capita income of Iraq, which is major oil- producing and exporting country, with a very large oil reserve along with a high production capacity of over 3 million barrel/ day, should have maintain a much higher income than that shown in Table 3 of only $3600 in 2008. This very low figure caused by a special, peculiar case; came as a result of the Iraqi war with the present U.S. government. Their GDP per capita income is expected to surely surge upon the cessation of this disastrous war and establishment of peace in the country.

Table 3 – Arab Countries per Capita Income (PPP)

Rank	Country	2004	2005	2006	2007	2008
	Qatar***	68,166	70,772	76,537	80,870*	84,833*
	Kuwait***	35,978	36,953	38,072*	39,306*	40,875*
	UAE***	30,954	32,751	35,882	37,293*	38,108*
	Bahrain	25,137	27,723	29,873	32,064*	34,043*
	Oman***	18,887	20,424	22,152	23,967*	26,023*
	Saudi Arabia***	19,487	21,236	22,290*	23,243*	24,240*
	Libya***	9,981	10,737	11,421	12,277*	13,361*
	Lebanon	10,206	10,499*	10,692*	11,270*	11,690*
	Tunisia	6,030	6,453	6,934*	7,473*	7,939*
	Algeria***	5,609	6,044	6,191	6,533*	6,885*
	Egypt**	4,466	4,714	5,094	5,491*	5,874*
	Jordan	4,016	4,297	4,606	4,886*	5,140*
	Syria**	3,945	4,130	4,311*	4,488*	4,648*
	Morocco	3,382	3,554*	3,922*	4,076*	4,385*
	Iraq***				3,600*	
	Yemen**	2,109	2,203	2,274	2,335*	2,406*
	Sudan**	1,645	1,755	1,964*	2,172*	2,322*
	Mauritania**	1,666	1,767*	1,984*	2,008*	2,123*
	Palestine			1,010*		

*Estimates

** Oil-producing country, capacity sufficient for local use, sparing some excess, less than one million barrel/day, for export

***Major producing and oil-exporting country

Table 3a – Arab World population and GDP by region

Region	Population	GDP (USD million)
Gulf Cooperation Council (GCC)	39,370,307	1,075,983
United Arab Maghreb (UAM)	86,608,356	389,643
Arab Mediterranean Union*	221,001,852	662,220
Oil Rich countries	106,240,071	1,426,630
Total Arab World	**328,801,172**	**1,914,172**

*Includes UAM

Table 3a shows the major parity – with large differences -in GDP of GCC countries of about 56% of total Arab world GDP compared to less than 12% of region's total population. By comparison both the 5 total Arab Maghreb- population ratio to total Arabs of 26% and 10 total Mediterranean Arab countries population ratio to total of 67%, each has only 20% and 34% of total region's GDP, respectively; for ratios see following Table 4. *(Again as concluded in a later section, this large GDP parity can be adjusted and greatly reduced by the establishment of AU).*

The witnessed sharp rise in cost of energy and the implication of that effect on price of many other life-essential commodities, which the Arab region has shortage in, and therefore they are large importer of these commodities. The price of these commodities   is expected to rise significantly as it already did, the price of some already doubled, now beyond the affordability of many people within the region. Buying power of region's currency is now regressing, making it very difficult for many of their people to buy their daily food. These nations are definitely greatly hurt by the high energy cost and its large effect on cost and price of essential commodities, many of which are imported by the region.

If the oil prices continue to maintain their present rise in future, the trend in rise of GDP per capita (PPP) income, already noticed in Table 3, for the 8 major oil-producing and export-ing Arab countries of: Qatar, Kuwait, United Arab Emirates, Oman, Saudi Arabia (Gulf Arab countries), Iraq, Libya, and Algeria, is expected to continue to rise [see Reference1], which shows also the countries respective world ranking of: 1, 10, 16, 38, 39, 62 and 94. This observed, upward rising trend in GDP income of major oil-rich exporting Arab countries has the reverse negative effect, as already indicated earlier, on their brethren, the poor Arab countries' population (as well as on all world poor nations' population) since rise in price of energy brings with it a huge rise in price of other commodities and services, which no longer can be afforded by a great segment of the poor Arab countries population and other poor nations of the world as well.

The above accelerated rise in GDP per capita income in Gulf Arab countries is expected to continue to rise as reported in Reference [11], where the GCC countries' total GDP of $340 billions in year 2002, reached $800 billions by the end of 2007 and is expected to reach $912 Billions by the end of year 2008! Definitely similar rise in GDP of the remaining major oil-producing and exporting countries of: Iraq, Libya and Algeria will occur. The present price of oil now about $70/barrel may or may-not support the above assumption. In spite of this great wealth the region is now under great stress when compared to developed or emerging nations /regions such as U.S., Japan or EU.

How about that: the unexpected astonishing rise in GDP income of major oil-producing and exporting Arab countries? "Would it be used unwisely as it was done in the past leaving the region non-industrialized, divided, non-coordinated, suffering from many conflicts without the freedom of thought and decision as is the case now, always under the dominance of mighty nations and geopolitical and economic conditions? Or should it be utilized wisely as proposed through out the text, accelerating the formation of the proposed "Arab Union", developing the R&D-based techno-economic plan to bring the Arab World region to advanced (developed) nations status, prestige, having freedom of thought and free decision, masters of their destiny and decision and having the ability to contribute to science and knowledge as their ancestors did during their Golden Age era (see also last part of the Introduction Section)?"

Finally, this section (Table 4) compares Arab countries' GDP to that of selected advanced world nations. The main objective of the comparison is to show first: how the total Arab market fairs and ranks in wealth compared to these selected advanced/emerging markets, and secondly, how it - their wealth - can be significantly improved as shown later throughout the proposal.

Table 4: Comparison of total Arab GDP income to that of selected advanced nations/regions

Country/Region	Population (millions)	GDP (USD billions)	GDP Per Capita	Wealth Ratio
Section A				
Arab World- total	329	1,914	5,818	1.00
Gulf Cooperation Council	39	1,075	27,284	0.56
Oil Rich Arab' countries	106	1,426	13,427	0.75
Union of the Mediterranean	221	662	2,496	0.35
United Arab Maghreb	87	390	4,498	0.20
Section B				
European Union	495	18,394	37,137	9.61
USA	307	14,265	46,561	7.46
Japan	127	4,923	38,612	2.57
Germany	82	3,676	44,610	1.92
UK	62	2,674	43,409	1.40
France	65	2,868	44,022	1.50
China	1,332	4,402	3,305	2.33
Arab World	329	1,914	5,818	1.00

The list includes the GDP of several selected advanced nations, many of which have extensive area of land, either unionized, part of a union or they possess large, free and highly advanced/emerging markets, and how it - their GDP and wealth – compares to that of Arab countries. The various regions/nations differ as shown in Table 4 in population as well as in their GDP income. The present GDP wealth ratio of: 9.61, 7.46, 2.57, 2.23, 1.92, 1.5 and 1.4 for the European Union, U.S.A, Japan, China, Germany, France and U.K, respectively, are compared to the ratio of Arab World's wealth which is set to a ratio of 1.00. When these ratios are adjusted for population, they are raised to: 7.68, 7.48, 7.58 and 6.62 for Germany, U.K, France and Japan, respectively. Implementation of the EU and U.S. unions or having huge open markets, they all were able to greatly exceed the Arab countries wealth by 9.61 and 7.4 fold, while China exceeded it by 2.23 fold. This excess wealth came as a result in their difference with Arab countries in that: these various regions have either a union with huge cooperative, coordinated open common market or nations have an open large combative market and in both cases the market is combined with advanced industry - an advanced high tech one. In all cases, these unions and markets are strongly supported by rigid application of the R&D-based techno-economic plans, which is completely ignored by nearly all the Arab regions. *(Similar adoption of these acts as given in our proposal makes it possible and achievable for the Arab world to reduce this wealth ratio significantly and raise their population's standard of living and quality of life).*

...   .

References

1. International Monetary Fund, world economic outlook database, April, 2008.

2. Euro to Dollar Exchange Rate 2000-2005.

3. September 2000 UNITED NATIONS MILLENNIUM DECLARATION.

4. Geneva, 9 January 2002 — the United Nations Millennium Summit.

5. Ata M Hassan, the Blue Revolution, San Diego, 2006.

6. President Clinton's Global Initiative, 2005.

7. Africa Turn, A New Green Revolution for the 21st Century, The Rockefeller Foundation, 2006.

8. G8 Summit in Gleneagles, Scotland 2005.

9. G8 Summit in Heiligendamm, Germany, June 2007.

10. List of countries by GDP (nominal) per capita, From Wikipedia, the free encyclopedia, 2007.

11. Qatar's per capita income more than US, http://www.freshplaza.com.

Chapter 3 - R&D in Developed and Developing Nations

Through the ages, the human race has introduced a great number of technological revolutions; many of which generated tremendous benefits to humanity. They blossomed from discoveries and structured proven R&D processes which are supported with ample capital investment. Needless to say the R&D processes resulted in groundbreaking technological and economical innovations; the current Information Technology Revolution being a classic example. Further more, by their continuous use, they contributed immensely toward the nation's advancement to their present healthy, wealthy and progressive nations' status.

One of the greatest R&D achievements (1942-1960) was the Green Revolution (GRRV), which way back stymied an imminent wave of starvation through improved food (cereals) production methods [1]. Presently, world food shortage is being highly exaggerated, doubling of cereal prices worldwide, making food prices far beyond affordability by many poor nations. The surge in price of cereals came as a result of the spectacular surge in price of energy. To offset the rise in price of energy a good portion of the grains, which make a major part of humane and animal food, is being wastefully used in making insufficient fuel additive, a questionable low priority use compared to that as a life-essential substance. This adverse effect necessitates further R&D efforts on the revival of the GRRV as it is being introduced now in Africa. This act is being conducted on the addition of the huge R&D efforts being done now and future on to develop environmentally clean, alternative sources of energy as well as other human, animal and plant requirements.

A basic need, water is now facing the same dilemma; it is in severe shortage supply in many parts of the world. In turn the water shortage contributes to food shortage, since water (together with sun and air) is very essential for agriculture and food production. The "Blue Revolution" was recently introduced by the author to reverse the course of water and food shortages around the globe through the applications of R&D technology to service humanity with the development of new innovative and improved seawater desalination process technologies in its international R&D institutes, to produce fresh water from the sea in abundance at reduced cost and to avail the technology free of charge to all humanity who needs it [2]. Realization of the

BLRV should assist sustain the world's industrial growth. Another important objective of the BLRV is to augment and sustain the yield of the GRRV by increasing food production. Such R&D efforts are timely and are of great significance, especially when nearly one half of the world population is expected to live by the year 2025 within 50 miles from the sea coast.

Governments, corporations, private companies and venture capitalists are now working on development of nanotechnology and Stem Cell research as they believe that both shall provide the next wave of innovation by the investment of over $10 billion in year 2004 alone [3]. More than $8.6 billion were spent in the year 2004 on R&D in nanotechnology and nano-science by governments (about $3.6 billion), corporations (about $4 billion), and venture capitalists which invested about $1 billion. Many of the world advanced nations expect the nanotechnology to mark the on setting of a surprising second industrial revolution, where materials can be produced with fantastic, much superior properties than their present counterparts.

A huge number of R&D activities, which are heavily funded, are being conducted worldwide. The total global spending on R&D topped $1 trillion in year 2006, which is expected soon to rise significantly to meet the very large R&D expenditure in search of alternative, low cost sources of energy, to be spent mainly by the advanced nations and with very insignificant amounts being spent by the non-developed ones that are now badly in need of developing technology. Alone, the U.S.A. total 2007 R&D budget expenditure for both the government and private sectors is $338 billion, compared to $136.8 billion for China, now the second world largest in this field[4,5]. All advanced nations are heavily engaged in R&D efforts and as shown later spend considerable sum of their GDP on R&D activities. Publications and R&D efforts are quite extensive and only limited references are given here for illustration [5-10].

Table1 shows the key indicators on world population, GDP, total R&D spending and ratio to GDP for developed, developing and less developing nations for the year 2002. Developed countries spent a total of $645.8 billions of world total of $829 billions or 77.8% of world total, as compared to $183.6 billions or 22.1%, and $0.5 billions or 0.1% of world total, spent respectively by developing and less developing nations. The three continents: North America Europe and Asia's accounted for R&D spending of $307, $226.2 and $261.5 or 37%, 27.3% and 31.5%, respectively, for a total of 95.8% of world total. The remaining 4.2% was spent by the rest of the world countries, where the total Arab World countries accounted for a meager value of only $1.9 billions or 0.2%! The % GDP ratio for selected world countries and their %GDP ratio are as shown in same table [11]. The U.S. R&D's spending amounted to 35% compared to 12.8% and 8.7% of world total for Japan and China, respectively (Table 1).

Table 1
KEY INDICATORS ON WORLD GDP, POPULATION AND GERD, 2002

	GDP (in billions)	% world GDP	Population (in millions)	% world population	GERD (in billions)	% world GERD	% GERD /GDP	GERD per inhabitant
World	47 599.4	100.0	6 176.2	100.0	829.9	100.0	1.7	134.4
Developed countries	28 256.5	59.4	1 195.1	19.3	645.8	77.8	2.3	540.4
Developing countries	18 606.5	39.1	4 294.2	69.5	183.6	22.1	1.0	42.8
Less-developed countries	736.4	1.5	686.9	11.1	0.5	0.1	0.1	0.7
Americas	14 949.2	31.4	849.7	13.8	328.8	39.6	2.2	387.0
North America	11 321.6	23.8	319.8	5.2	307.2	37.0	2.7	960.5
Latin America and the Caribbean	3 627.5	7.6	530.0	8.6	21.7	2.6	0.6	40.9
Europe	13 285.8	27.9	795.0	12.9	226.2	27.3	1.7	284.6
European Union	10 706.4	22.5	453.7	7.3	195.9	23.6	1.8	431.8
Comm. of Ind. States in Europe	1 460.0	3.1	207.0	3.4	17.9	2.2	1.2	86.6
Central, Eastern and Other Europe	1 119.4	2.4	134.4	2.2	12.4	1.5	1.1	92.6
Africa	1 760.0	3.7	832.2	13.4	4.6	0.6	0.3	5.6
Sub-Saharan countries	1 096.9	2.3	644.0	10.4	3.5	0.4	0.3	5.5
Arab States Africa	663.1	1.4	188.2	3.0	1.2	0.1	0.2	6.5
Asia	16 964.9	35.6	3 667.5	59.4	261.5	31.5	1.5	71.3
Comm. of Ind. States in Asia	207.9	0.4	72.6	1.2	0.7	0.1	0.4	10.3
Newly Indust. Asia	2 305.5	4.8	374.6	6.1	53.5	6.4	2.3	142.8
Arab States Asia	556.0	1.2	103.9	1.7	0.6	0.1	0.1	6.2
Other Asia	1 720.0	3.6	653.7	10.6	1.4	0.2	0.1	2.1
Oceania	639.5	1.3	31.8	0.5	8.7	1.1	1.4	274.2
Other groupings								
Arab States All	1 219.1	2.6	292.0	4.7	1.9	0.2	0.2	6.4
Comm. of Ind. States All	1 667.9	3.5	279.6	4.5	18.7	2.2	1.1	66.8
OECD	28 540.0	60.0	1 144.1	18.5	655.1	78.9	2.3	572.6
Selected countries								
Argentina	386.6	0.8	36.5	0.6	1.6	0.2	0.4	44.0
Brazil*	1 300.3	2.7	174.5	2.8	13.1	1.6	1.0	75.0
China	5 791.7	12.2	1 280.4	20.7	72.0	8.7	1.2	56.2
Egypt*	252.9	0.5	66.4	1.1	0.4	0.1	0.2	6.6
France	1 608.8	3.4	59.5	1.0	35.2	4.2	2.2	591.5
Germany	2 226.1	4.7	82.5	1.3	56.0	6.7	2.5	678.3
India*	2 777.8	5.8	1 048.6	17.0	20.8	2.5	0.7	19.8
Israel	124.8	0.3	6.6	0.1	6.1	0.7	4.9	922.4
Japan	3 481.3	7.3	127.2	2.1	106.4	12.8	3.1	836.6
Mexico	887.1	1.9	100.8	1.6	3.5	0.4	0.4	34.7
Russian Federation	1 164.7	2.4	144.1	2.3	14.7	1.8	1.3	102.3
South Africa	444.8	0.9	45.3	0.7	3.1	0.4	0.7	68.7
United Kingdom	1 574.5	3.3	59.2	1.0	29.0	3.5	1.8	490.4
United States of America	10 414.3	21.9	288.4	4.7	290.1	35.0	2.8	1005.9

* GERD figures for Brazil, India and Egypt are all for 2000.
Note: For Asia, the sub-regional totals do not include China, India or Japan in any of the tables in the present chapter.

Source: UNESCO Institute for Statistics estimations, December 2004.

Table 2 lists the Worldwide R&D Expenditure as % of Nation's GDP for the 4 consecutive years 2002 – 2005 [12], while the ranking of the first 20 leading nations, arranged according to their total expenditure (in U.S dollar) on R&D activities for the year 2005 or 2004, is discussed in the following section. The highly industrial advanced techno-economic countries, such as North America and Western Europe and other countries in East Asia and the Pacific-specifically Japan,

China, S. Korea and other Asia Pacific region countries, spend a good % of their GDP up to 3% and some higher ratio on R&D work. Majority of nations, especially in Africa, great numbers in Asia, South America and other parts of the world including Arab World countries spend very insignificant (%) of their GPD on R&D activities. The R&D spending by Central and Eastern European countries is lesser than that of western European nations; it ranges between about 0.5 to 1.5%.   Many of world countries (about 125 including 14 Arab countries), their names are taken out from the table, since they fail to provide information on the subject, either because they maintained   no R&D activity or whatever activity they have is impressively insignificant, not worthily of reporting! A total of 35   countries whose R&D spending was less than 0.35% of GDP for a total of 160 countries, their names were also dropped from the list.

Table 2 - Worldwide R&D Expenditure of more than 0.35 % of Nation's GDP (Source: UNESCO Institute for Statistics – 2008)[1],2

Arab States	2002	2003	2004	2005
Morocco	0.62	0.75	...	...
Tunisia	0.63	0.73	1.00	1.03

North America & Europe	2002	2003	2004	2005
Austria	2.12	2.20	2.21	2.35
Belgium	1.94	1.89	1.86	1.82
Canada	2.07	2.03	2.05	2.01
Cyprus	0.31	0.35	0.38	0.40
Denmark	2.51	2.56	2.48	2.45
Finland	3.43	3.48	3.51	3.52
France	2.23	2.17	2.14	2.13
Germany	2.49	2.52	2.49	2.51
Greece	...	0.63	0.61	0.61
Iceland	3.01	2.87	2.82	...
Ireland	1.10	1.16	1.20	1.24
Israel	5.04	4.66	4.63	4.95
Italy	1.13	1.11	1.10	...
Luxembourg	...	1.66	1.65	1.56
Malta	0.27	0.27	0.64	0.61
Netherlands	1.72	1.76	1.79	...
Norway	1.67	1.73	1.62	1.51
Portugal	0.76	0.74	0.77	0.81
Spain	0.99	1.05	1.07	1.12
Sweden	...	3.95	...	3.86
Switzerland	...	...	2.94	...
United Kingdom	1.83	1.79	1.75	...
United States	2.65	2.68	2.68	...

Continuation of Table 2

East Asia Pacific	2002	2003	2004	2005
Australia	1.69	...	1.77	...
China	1.07	1.13	1.23	1.34
Hong Kong (China), SAR	0.59	0.69	0.74	...
Japan	3.18	3.20	3.18	...
Malaysia	0.69	...	0.63	...
New Zealand	...	1.14	...	...
Singapore	2.15	2.12	2.24	2.36
Central Europe Central /Eastern Europe	2002	2003	2004	2005
Belarus	0.62	0.61	0.63	0.69
Bulgaria	0.49	0.50	0.51	0.50
Croatia	1.11	1.11	1.22	...
Czech Republic	1.20	1.25	1.26	1.42
Estonia	0.75	0.82	0.91	0.99
Hungary	1.01	0.94	0.89	0.95
Latvia	0.42	0.38	0.42	0.57
Lithuania	0.66	0.67	0.76	0.76
Poland	0.56	0.54	0.56	0.57
Romania	0.38	0.39	0.39	...
Russian Federation	1.25	1.28	1.16	1.07
Serbia and Montenegro	1.18	1.24	1.37	1.41
Slovakia	0.58	0.58	0.53	0.52
Slovenia	1.52	1.32	1.45	1.22
Turkey	0.66	0.61	0.67	...
Ukraine	1.00	1.11	1.08	1.07

Central Asia	2002	2003	2004	2005
South and West Asia	2002	2003	2004	2005
India	0.69	0.65	0.63	0.61
Iran, Islamic Republic of	0.55	0.67	0.59	...
Pakistan	0.22	...	...	0.43
Sri Lanka	...	...	0.19	...

Latin America / Caribbean	2002	2003	2004	2005
Argentina	0.39	0.41	0.44	...
Brazil	1.00	0.97	0.91	...
Chile	0.68	0.67	0.68	...
Costa Rica	...	0.36	0.37	...
Cuba	0.53	0.54	0.56	...
Mexico	0.44	0.43	0.41	...

Continuation of Table 2

Sub-Saharan Africa	2002	2003	2004	2005
Democratic Republic of the Congo	...	...	0.42	0.48
Mauritius	0.39	0.35	0.40	0.38
Mozambique	0.52	...	...	...
Seychelles	0.41	0.41	0.41	0.40
South Africa	...	0.80	0.87	...
Uganda	0.98	1.05	1.16	1.25

[1]. Source: UNESCO Institute for Statistics – 2008[12].

The above great differences in R&D spending between the developed advanced   and developing, less advanced nations (Tables 1 and 2) raises the question: "why all this great spending worldwide by advanced nations on R&D efforts and why not to save the money, the way it is now done by the developing and under developed, less advanced nations, including the Arab world countries?" All of us know that in this 21 century the wealth of nations and their well-being is to a great extent tied   to their spending on developing the technology in order to maintain and improve on development of their science, technology and the overall economy/industry [4-10]. The advanced nations now spend a good percentage of their GDP (up to 3%, some more up to 5%) on such R&D programs. To them the R&D spending is neither a luxury nor astounding or astonishing act. Rather, it is very essential and necessary for the maintenance and growth of their high tech industrial economy.

Innovation through R&D is also essential in order to protect, expand and improve their trading share in world market place as well as provide them the means of identifying new knowledge and therefore new markets. Those maters, although are exceedingly important to the health and well being of nation's economy, for one reason or another, they are surprisingly not followed by the non-developed nations including Arab countries. Some authority needs to remind them, including of course first the Arab countries, that they are living now in a century where R&D spending is not only important to advance their economy and overall status but also should be given the top, top priority to all other activities, with R&D in the necessary life-essentials substances toping the priority list.

Principally, as already indicated, because of the above mentioned phenomena, the nations of the world are classified into have (advanced) and have-not (underdeveloped) nations, see Chapter 2. Contrary to the developed nations' success story, a great majority of developing' world nations, their economic/industrial plans were void of such scientific, technical R&D programs, the lack of which failed them to attain an advanced, developed nation status. They spent very little on R&D activity and with their majority having no R&D budget at all (Table 2). Historically, no great progress was experienced in the economies of many developing nations, some of them have regressed. Unfortunately the Arab region continues to be among the underdeveloped nations; they have allocated very little, some none, investment on R&D work. By doing so they deprived their economy/industry the chance to grow, industrialize, progress and kept many of their nations suffering from extreme poverty and backwardness as well.

3.1 Advanced Nations Expenditure on R&D Activities

Table 3 shows the 20 top leaders in expenditure on R&D activities worldwide and how much each of these developed nations spent on R&D activities (Years 2004 or 2005) in term of on R&D (US$) and % ratio of this sum to the country's GDP [11-12]. Table 4 shows the same for year 2007 but ranking nation's R&D spending first according to total expenditure in US$ followed second by its % of GDP. Figure 1 shows the top 20 nations' R&D expenditure for year 2007 as percentage of their GDP. For comparison the Arab World contribution to their R&D efforts are shown in both Tables 3 and Figure 1. Meanwhile Table 3 shows also the Source of Funds (%): from Business Enterprise or from Government and the per capita spent by that nation on R&D. Although only 20 names are given in the table, Table 2 shows the percentage of country GDP spent on R&D activities by many countries of the world. Nations with the richest economies spent the highest sum but not necessarily as shown below the highest GDP % ratio. The R&D spending in U.S dollars increases with nation's wealth and their economy size; nations with the richest economies spent the highest values. By far U.S. the wealthiest nation worldwide, spends the largest sum followed by Japan, then the second wealthiest nation, China and Germany, although as shown in later sections, in year 2006 China replaced Japan as second ranked nation In terms of R&D expenditure.

The top 20 leading R&D nations in terms of US$ R&D expenditure are not necessarily ranked also as the top 20 in terms of their R&D funding as percent GDP ratio (see Table 4). Both, Israel with 4.95% and Sweden with 3.86% of their GDP spent on R&D, ranked number I and 2, although, because of the size of their economy, they ranked much higher -15 and 13th -in terms of (US$) Expenditure on R&D. Other nations that spend high (%) of GDP on R&D are Japan (3.18%) and republic of South Korea (2.99%) compared to (2.68%) and (2.51%) for U.S.A and Germany, respectively. Other nations Percentage of GDP expenditure on R&D activity is shown in the same table. Among the 20th top R&D spenders, the 5 highest US$ per capita R&D spenders of: $1317, $1252, $1132, $1058 and $1024 are Israel, Sweden, Finland, United States and Switzerland, respectively.

Source of (%) funding of R&D expenditure from Business Enterprise varies from 74%, 69.1%, and 67% in Japan, Switzerland, and China, respectively, to 63.7% in U.S.A, and a much lower ratio in other European countries. The situation is reversed for (%) government funding in other countries where the highest funding of: 75.3%, 62% and 57.9% were in India, Russian Federation and Brazil, respectively. Evidently higher % funding ratio by Business Enterprise exist in other

Table 3 - Top 20 Countries, Ranked According to their Expenditure on R&D

Country	Year	R&D Expenditure US$	% of GDP	Per Capita (US$)	Source of Funds (%) - Business Enterprise	Source of Funds (%) - Government
United States of America	2004	312,535,430	2.68%	1058.0	63.7%	31.0%
Japan	2004	120,261,833	3.18%	940.1	74.8%	18.1%
China	2005	117,957,063	1.34%	89.6	67.0%	26.3%
Germany	2005	60,925,969	2.51%	736.8	...	...
France	2005	39,367,959	2.13%	650.8	...	...
U. Kingdom	2004	33,317,581	1.75%	560.2	44.2%	32.8%
India	2005	22,924,827	0.61%	20.8	19.8%	75.3%
Canada	2005	21,703,417	2.01%	672.6	47.9%	23.9%
Italy	2004	17,831,149	1.10%	307.3	...	...
Russian Federation	2005	16,583,964	1.07%	115.8	30.0%	62.0%
Brazil	2004	13,558,605	0.91%	73.7	39.9%	57.9%
Spain	2005	13,168,522	1.12%	305.8	...	...
Sweden	2005	11,322,409	3.86%	1252.3	...	...
Australia	2004	10,797,961	1.77%	541.5	51.6%	39.8%
Netherlands	2004	9,139,619	1.79%	563.3	...	...
Israel	2005	8,858,822	4.95%	1317.4	...	...
Switzerland	2004	7,416,202	2.94%	1024.4	69.7%	22.7%
Austria	2005	6,520,837	2.35%	796.2	45.7%	36.4%
Belgium	2005	6,126,416	1.82%	588.0	...	...
Finland	2005	5,944,380	3.52%	1132.5	...	...
Arab World			0.2%			

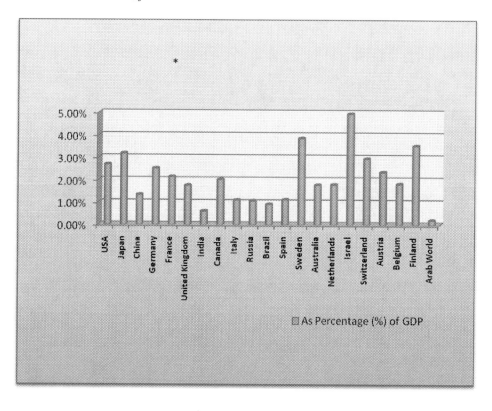

Figure1: Top 20 Nations R&D Expenditure as Percentage of GDP

Table 4 - 2007 Top 20 List of Countries by GDP and Expenditure on R&D
(Source: UNESCO Institute for Statistics – 2008)

Rank	Country	GDP (US$ Millions)	Country	R&D Expenditure (US$ Million)	% of GDP
1	USA	13,843,825	USA	312,535,430	2.68%
2	Japan	4,383,762	Japan	120,261,833	3.18%
3	Germany	3,322,147	China	117,957,063	1.34%
4	China	3,250,827	Germany	60,925,969	2.51%
5	UK	2,772,570	France	39,367,959	2.13%
6	France	2,560,255	UK	33,317,581	1.75%
7	Italy	2,104,666	India	22,924,827	0.61%
8	Spain	1,438,959	Canada	21,703,417	2.01%
9	Canada	1,432,140	Italy	17,831,149	1.10%
10	Brazil	1,313,590	Russian Federation	16,583,964	1.07%
11	Russia	1,289,582	Brazil	13,558,605	0.91%
12	India	1,098,945	Spain	13,168,522	1.12%
13	South Korea	957,053	Sweden	11,322,409	3.86%
14	Australia	908,826	Australia	10,797,961	1.77%
15	Mexico	893,365	Netherlands	9,139,619	1.79%
16	Netherlands	768,704	Israel	8,858,822	4.95%
17	Turkey	663,419	Switzerland	7,416,202	2.94%
18	Sweden	455,319	Austria	6,520,837	2.35%
19	Belgium	453,636	Belgium	6,126,416	1.82%
20	Indonesia	432,944	Finland	5,944,380	3.52%

Source: 2007 List by the International Monetary Fund

countries dominated by large, high capital free enterprise industries, while high government funding is done in countries with less of large capital free enterprise industries, largely controlled, owned or dominated by the government, which themselves are in support and strong funding of R&D efforts to promote and revive the nation' economy.

For brevity, only 4 cases of leading R&D nations or union of nations: are discussed in brief, while R&D in Arab World is drawn for comparison since it represents the case for R&D activities in developing region or country. These 5 cases should suffice to illustrate the significance and importance of the issue to the health, well being of a country/region techno-economic and industrialization plan and status. These cases are: U.S.A (United Federated States) followed second by the European Union then China, Japan trailed by the Arab World nations. The two nations of China and Japan are ranked as second and third countries to U.S in spending worldwide in terms of U.S Dollars spent during the same year on R&D activities.

3.1.1 R&D in USA

The U.S.A is the largest worldwide nation in the wealth of economy, leads the world in (US$) Expenditure on R&D activities as well (Tables 3 and 4). The U.S.A is/was well-known as an industrial nation with an R&D budget that had shown through the years a tremendous increase from as little as $12 Billion in 1959 to $284 in the year 2003, far beyond any expectation, even when accounting for inflation effects. By the year 2004 the total R&D spending reached USD $290.83 billion or about 2.7% of the 2004 country's GDP [5]. The R&D budget is highly diversified: total federal government, private industry, academia and other non-profit R&D agencies spent, respectively, the sum of $26.09, $198.1, $50.74 and $15.9 billions of current (2004) U.S. dollars. Portions of this R&D budget of $57.7, $69.6 and $163.5 billions of 2004 US dollars were spent on conducting basic research, applied research and development research, respectively. In dollar value, the 2004 total US R&D budget was more than three times the total 2004 budget of the Saudi Arabian government of only USD $89.9 billion. There is no need to compare it to that of other Arab countries such as Egypt or Jordan or others; the comparison would be astounding. In spite of its large quantity, the forecast of total funding for research and development in USA was increased to $338 billion in 2007, an increase of 2.85 percent over the $329 billion funded in 2006 and over 16% during the last three years when compared to R&D spending for the year 2004, or an increase of about 5.4% per year [4, 5]! With the high emphasis now on multiplication of alternative energy sources and food production the total R&D budget is expected to rise significantly in both USD$ value and as percentage (%) of GDP. The requirement for the expansion is now recognized by all U.S. parties, the private and government sectors as well.

As is the case with other nations concerned with the advantage and prestige of innovation, the overall increase in U.S.A R&D budget is driven by industry funding (63.7% in 2004) and industrial, product innovation and performance. According to Jules Duga "Overriding all themes in this year's forecast are the dual needs of growing and maintaining the strong technological base that has characterized the U.S. for over 50 years and assuring that the education system provides the critical raw material for the engine that operates our industrial base" [4].

Definitely technology-based industries in U.S, and elsewhere in advanced countries, spent large sum of money on funding their R&D work; the spending is very essential. For example, some of the high tech industry, such as the recently highly developed chip and information industries, and pharmaceutical companies spend a large sum of their total company sale on R&D work, some times in excess of 20%. Nearly, all U.S.A. industries are engaged in R&D activities.

3.1.2 R&D in the European Union

Table 5 shows the preliminary results of R&D expenditure in the EU27 (for then 27 member states) as percentage of EU GDP in year 2001-2005 and also in terms of million current Euros in year 2005 [8]. The data is arranged in terms of the increasing R&D expenditure ratio to the R&D expenditure is expressed in million current U.S $. (Information comes from Reference: STAT/07/6 Date: 12/01/2007, of Euro stat, the Statistical Office of the European Communities country's GPD). First in GDP% is the Scandinavian region, followed second by the 6 countries that initiated the European Common Market and then by the remaining EU27 including the central and eastern Europe member countries, which tend to be the lowest in their R&D expenditure and activities. The final section of the table compares the EU27 R&D expenditure ratio to that spent by the leading worldwide R&D spenders (in U.S. dollar) of U.S, Japan and China.

The average R&D expenditure of all the EU27 as percentage of EU GDP and also in terms of total euro in year 2001-2005 were respectively at 1.84%, the same as in 2004, and just over 200 billion euro (equals 316 billion USD$ at the present euro/$ ratio of about 1.58). The R&D intensity, however, remained significantly lower in the EU27 than that in other major economies. In 2004, R&D expenditure was 2.68% of GDP in the United States, 3.18% in Japan, while it has reached 1.34% in China in 2005. The R&D expenditure grew by 1.5% per year between 2001 and 2005 as compared to 1.7% in the United States and 2.0% in Japan between 2001 and 2004. Also, in 2004 the business sector financed 55% of total EU27 R&D expenditure, which was less than that ratio of 64% in the United States and considerably less than it was 75% in Japan and 66% in China.

In terms of total euro R&D expenditure in the EU27 in 2005, the highest spenders in billion Euros were Germany (56.4), France (36.4), U.K. (30.4), Italy (15.3), Sweden (11.1) and Spain (10.1). These values compare to other major economies in billions of U.S dollars spent on R&D activities of: 312, 120 and 118, by U.S, Japan, and China, respectively.

In 2005, the R&D intensity varies from (about 0.4% in 2004)   of GDP in Cyprus and Romania to high value of 3.9% in Sweden. The highest R&D intensities among the Member States were registered in: Sweden (3.86% of GDP) and Finland (3.48%), followed by Germany (2.51%), Denmark (2.44%), Austria (2.36%) and France (2.13%). The lowest intensities were found in Romania (0.39% in 2004), Cyprus (0.40%), Bulgaria (0.50%) and Slovakia (0.51%) and other Easter European nations.

Annual average growth rates of R&D expenditure in real terms over the period 2001 to 2005 ranged from +18% in Latvia, +17% in Estonia, +15% in Cyprus, +11% in Lithuania, -2% in Belgium and Slovenia, and -1% in Slovakia.

Table 5 - Research and Development Expenditure in the EU

	R&D Expenditure as % of GDP million current Euros			R&D Expenditure		R&D Expenditure Financed by Business (%)
	2001	2004	2005	2005 (Euro)	Growth %	2004
EU27	1.88	1.84	1.84	201 020	1.5	54.9
Original 6 EU Nations						
Germany	2.46	2.50	2.51p	56 356p	1.0	66.8
France	2.20	2.14	2.13p	36 396p	0.6	51.7
Italy	1.09	1.10	:	15 253*	0.8	:
Netherlands	1.80	1.78p	:	8 723*p	0.4	51.1**
Belgium	2.08	1.85p	1.82p	5 428p	-1.7	60.3**
Luxembourg	1.65****	1.66	1.56p	458p	1.8	80.4
Scandinavian Countries						
Sweden	4.25	:	3.86	11 109	0.2	65.0**
Finland	3.30	3.46	3.48	5 474	3.8	69.3
Denmark	2.39	2.48p	2.44p	5 097p	2.1	59.9**
Norway	1.60	1.62	1.51p	3 599p	0.5	49.2**
Iceland	2.98	2.83	:	297*	1.5	43.9**
Other European Countries						
Austria	2.04p	2.23	2.36p	5 784p	5.4	47.2
United Kingdom	1.83	1.73	:	29 956*	0.7	44.2
Ireland	1.10p	1.21p	1.25p	2 020p	8.5	57.2p
Portugal	0.80	0.77p	0.81p	1 189p	0.4	31.7**
Greece	0.64	0.61p	0.61p	1 112p	3.2	28.2**
Spain	0.91	1.06	1.12p	10 100p	8.4	48.0
Cyprus	0.25	0.37	0.40p	54p	15.2	18.9
Malta	:	0.63	0.61p	27p	:	18.6***
Eastern European Countries						
Bulgaria	0.47	0.51	0.50	106	6.8	28.2
Czech Republic	1.20	1.26	1.42	1 417	8.3	52.8
Estonia	0.71	0.88	0.94p	104p	16.5	36.5
Latvia	0.41	0.42	0.57	73	17.6	46.3
Lithuania	0.67	0.76	0.76	157	11.4	19.9
Hungary	0.92	0.88	0.94	838	5.0	37.1
Poland	0.62	0.56	0.57	1 386	1.1	26.9
Romania	0.39	0.39	:	235*	:	44.0
Slovenia	1.55	1.45	1.22	338	-2.3	58.5
Slovakia	0.63	0.51	0.51	194	-0.6	38.3
Croatia	1.11***	1.22	:	345*	9.5	43.0
Turkey	0.72	:	:	1 280***	-1.0	41.3***
Top 3 Nations based upon R&D spending						
China	0.95	1.23	1.34	118000	19.7	65.7
Japan	3.13	3.18	:	120000	2.0	74.8
United States	2.76	2.68p	:	312000 254p*	1.7	63.7p

: Data not available

P: estimated or provisional data

Presently, the business sector finances contribute the highest share of EU27 expenditure on R&D (55%), which is for many members is below what other advanced countries spend on R&D activities. The government sector R&D expenditure is (35%) and funding from abroad only (8%). Among Member States, Luxembourg (80%) recorded the largest share of R&D expenditure financed by the business sector in 2004, followed by Finland (69%), Germany (67%), Sweden (65%), Belgium and Denmark (both 60%). Three Member States registered shares for the business sector of 20% or less: Malta and Cyprus (both 19%) and Lithuania (20%). In general, the R&D expenditure for many EU' members is below that of spending by many other advanced countries.

The R&D intensity is quite low in many of EU countries especially the countries of Eastern Europe (see Table 4) are below that of other advanced economies. To correct the situation, the Lisbon summit strategy set the EU goals in Research and Development to achieve by 2010 a R&D intensity of at least 3% for the EU as a whole from 1.84% in 2005, and to have two thirds of R&D expenditure financed by the business sector from its present ratio of about 55% in 2005. The ambitious goal was set also to allow EU countries to grow and to compete worldwide scientifically, technologically and economically at the same pace as other highly advanced economies.

(This should be a lesson to the Arab World and other underdeveloped regions to follow if they want their economy to grow and prosper resulting in an overall improvement of their people living standards and governments as well).

3.1.3 R&D in China

China's expenditure on R&D reached 60 billion US dollars in 2001, only after the United States and Japan of 282 billion and 104 billion dollars, respectively. China's spending accounted for 1.1 percent of its gross domestic products (GDP) that year, much higher than the 0.6 percent in 1996. About 40 percent of China's expenditure on research and development in 2001 was covered by the government and the rest 60 percent came from domestic and foreign enterprises. By the year 2003 China has 743,000 people involved in research and development activities compared to 1.3 million in US and 648,000 staff in Japan. In year 2004, China R&D spending was just over 1.2 percent of the country GDP. The OECD report attributed China's growing expenditures on R&D to the country's increasing investment in core technologies. There was a major rise in R&D budget from just over US $17 billion in 1995 to US $94 billion in 2004 (a 5.5 fold increase!), to reach US$136 billion in 2006 (an 8 fold increase!). The great increase in China R&D expenditure followed and was justified by the nation's great industrial and economic expansion. **(Again this should be a very great lesson to the Arab World and other underdeveloped regions to follow if they want their economy to grow and prosper**

resulting in an overall improvement of their people living standards and governments as well).

According to a recent report by the Organization for Economic Cooperation and Development (OECD) [13-16], in 2006 China invested a total of US$136 billion, replacing Japan, globally ranking second place after US in total amount of money spent on R&D activities. While the United States still has a bigger share of the global R&D market, second-ranked China have upped their investments in recent years, as reported in a new report conducted by *R&D* magazine and Battelle, a Columbus, Ohio-based research firm. In the year 2006, the United States R&D budget equaled 32.4% of the global R&D spending, but that number is down slightly from 32.7 percent in 2005, and is expected to drop to 31.9 percent of world R&D spending in year 2007. China ranks second for most dollars spent, and while it is only responsible for 13.4 percent of the world's R&D, Battelle projects that number will raise to 14.8 percent in 2007 and China is moving fast in this innovation arena. The percent changes may be small, but on a global scale, they translate into large figures.

In year 2006 as already mentioned, the global spending on R&D topped $1 trillion. Among other factors, the report explains the results in terms of an evolution in international competition: after the global arms race subsided, focus shifted to a "hands race" for lower-cost manual labor. Now shifting once again, the world is entering a "head and brains race" for technological advancement and China is heavily entering and engaged in the race.

With China leading the way, Asia continues to seize more and more of the international R & D market. Asia's share of global R&D grew from 34.9 percent in 2005 to 35.6 percent last year, and should continue to grow to a projected 36.5 percent in 2007 (**well, if these nations want to continue to grow and prosper they must raise their R&D efforts, a move unlike that followed by the Arab nations!**). Finally, in year 2008 China replaced Japan as the second richest country in the world behind the number one ranked: USA.

3.1.4 R&D in Japan

By comparison, spending in Japan on Research and Development is now the key to the countries' position as one of the highest, most advanced and developed nation worldwide, not only on technical aspects but also on the quality of their product as well [17-19]. As compared to the country's economy by the end of the Second World War, the damaged country's economy has matured and fantastically grown. By the years 1970- 1980, Japan gradually shifted away from dependence on foreign research by developing its ability to conduct independent research and development programs [19-21]. Obviously, this move was a very decisive factor in boosting the nation's competitiveness, and by doing so the government declared as early as year 1980 the commencement of "the era of Japan's technological independence". This move is a quite a drastic departure and transformation from where it was prior to world war two where the

Japanese industry were flooding the market place with their cheap products (as now the same is witnessed from some China's products). **(Again and again and again, this is a lesson to the Arab World and other underdeveloped regions to follow if they want their economy to grow and prosper resulting in an overall improvement of their people living standards and economy).**

By 1986 Japan had come to devote a higher % proportion of its GNP to research and development more than that ratio of the United States. In 1989 nearly 700,000 Japanese were engaged in research and development, more than the number of French, British, and West Germans combined. At the same time, Japan was producing more engineers than any country except the Soviet Union and the United States. Similar trends were seen in the use of capital resources. Japan spent US$ 39.1 billion on government and private research and development in 1987, equivalent to 2.9 percent of its national income (then, the highest ratio in the world). Although the United States spent around US$108.2 billion on research and development in 1987, only 2.6 percent of its GDP income was devoted to that purpose, ranking it third behind Japan and West Germany.

The Japanese reputation for originality also increased. Of the 1.2 million patents registered worldwide in 1985, 40 percent were Japanese, and Japanese citizens took out 19 percent of the 120,000 patent applications made in the United States. In 1987 around 33 percent of computer-related patents in the United States were Japanese, as were 30 percent of aviation-related patents and 26 percent of communications patents.

Despite its advances in technological research and development and its major commitment to applied research, however, Japan significantly trailed other industrialized nations in basic scientific research. In 1989 about 13 percent of Japanese research and development funds were devoted to basic research. The proportion of basic research expenses borne by government is also much lower in Japan than in the United States, as is Japan's ratio of basic research expenses to GNP. In the late 1980s, the Japanese government attempted to rectify national deficiencies in basic research by waging a broad "originality" campaign in schools, by generously funding research, and by encouraging private cooperation to do the same in various fields.

Most research and development is private (in year 2005 about 75% of R&D was financed by business sector), although government support to universities and laboratories aid industry was increased. In 1986 private industry provided 76 percent of the funding for research and development, which was especially strong in the late 1980s in electrical machinery (with a ratio of research costs to total sales of 5.5 percent in 1986), precision instruments (4.6 percent), chemicals (4.3 percent), and transportation equipment (3.2 percent).

As for government research and development, the national commitment to greater defense spending in the 1980s translated into increased defense-related research and development. Meanwhile, government moved away from supporting large-scale industrial technology, such as shipbuilding and steel. Research emphases in the 1980s were in alternative energy, information processing, life sciences, and modern industrial materials.

3.1.5 R&D in the Arab World Nations

Table2 lists the Worldwide R&D Expenditure as % of Nation's GDP for the 4 consecutive years 2002 – 2005, wherein to avoid   table clotting, the names of about 160, including 17 Arab countries, were taken out from the table, since the countries provided no information on the subject, either as mentioned, because they maintained   no R&D activity or whatever the activity they have are impressively insignificant, not worthily of reporting nor of great relevancy or fame to the nation progress! Table 6, taken from the same source shows the same for the Arab World countries, but with the various Arab countries names retained in the table as originally given in the information source, UNESCO Institute for Statistics, Table 2.

Table 6 - R&D Expenditure as % GDP of R&D in the Arab World Nations (Source: UNESCO Institute for Statistics – 2008)[12].

Year	2002	2003	2004	2005
Algeria	0.36	0.20	0.16	...
Bahrain	...	...	...	...
Djibouti	...	...	...	...
Egypt	...	...	...	...
Iraq	...	...	...	...
Jordan	0.34	...	...	...
Kuwait	0.18	...	...	...
Lebanon	...	...	...	...
Libyan Arab Jamahiriya	...	...	...	...
Mauritania	...	...	...	...
Morocco	0.62	0.75	...	...
Oman	...	...	...	...
Palestinian Autonomous Territories	...	...	...	...
Qatar	...	...	...	...
Saudi Arabia	...	...	...	...
Sudan	0.39	0.34	0.30	...
Syrian Arab Republic	...	...	...	...
Tunisia	0.63	0.73	1.00	1.03
United Arab Emirates	...	...	...	...
Yemen	...	...	...	...

Table 6 points out that of the total 20 Arab countries, 14 provided no information on the subject; only 6 countries provided information and only 1 of them (Tunisia), the information covered the 4 year range; the remaining 5 showed only partial coverage. The highest R&D Expenditure GDP ratio of 1.03% was again in Tunisia, which gradually increased its expenditure ratio, as it should, from 0.63% in 2001 to its highest value (1.03%) in 2005. The lowest GDP% ratio was in Algiers of 0.16% (see Table 6). With unavailability of information on the subject, it became also difficult to learn how much each of the various sectors, government, private enterprise companies, and other related institutions contributed to R&D funding. The lack of large free enterprise companies with a profit motive in the region (e.g., all the large oil companies are owned and controlled by the governments) tends to reveal and confirm that most of the R&D activities done in the region are government funded [20-25].

The severe shortage in providing R&D information indicates the irrelevancy of R&D works in the Arab world nations. Only an estimated 0.2 per cent of the Arab region's Gross Domestic Product is spent on scientific research (see Table 1) [11], while the United Nations average is estimated for the whole region is put at a slightly greater value at the meager ratio of a 0.5%, an amount that is still dwarfed by the much higher ratio shown earlier, between 2.7%, 3.18%,3.52%, 3.86% and 4.95% spent by the industrialized, high tech countries of United States , Japan, Finland, Switzerland and Israel, respectively. As shown in many of the earlier Tables 1-5 and Figure 1, many other nations also spend a much higher ratio on their R&D efforts than that spent by the Arab countries.

We see no reason for many of the Arab countries if not most of them to be in this awkward backward position, continuing to have a blind view of use of R&D technology in developing their region's economy/industry, although it was the attachment of their ancestors to knowledge and scholarship along with their union and huge open common market that gave birth to their "Golden Age Era" (750-1300), which allowed them also a top world position, ruling a great portion of the medieval world (see later Section 5.3.1). The same assumption applies to many other world developing regions [13-14].

With the exception of the will and determination, proper coordination, negotiation and compromise to perform this very important task, we believe they (the Arab countries) possess nearly all the necessary tools to perform this very important R&D-based techno-economic task. They have the capital plenty of it, especially now; the manpower, also plenty of it, which so far not efficiently utilized and with a large segment of it together with high percentage of the region' capital are exported to developed nations, mainly to the West. Besides, there is huge need of such potentially high tech manpower to solve through R&D work the many distressing problems, benefiting from the work of thousands of underutilized university graduate manpower.

There exists now urgent need for R&D work in the Arab region to perform multitude of activities in variety of fields to develop the necessary technology and tools to solve the many problems that kept the region behind. A summary list is given in Chapter 6, Section 6.6 [26-28] on how to increase and greatly enhance R&D efforts, intensity and funding at a fast pace in the region that badly need it.

...   .

References

1. Africa Turn, A New Green Revolution for the 21st Century, The Rockefeller Foundation, 2006.

2. Ata M Hassan, a Blue Revolution Book, San Diego, CA, U.S.A.

3. ibid, see pages 1 and 6 of above reference 1.

4. Dr. Jules Duga and Tim Studt, Battle, Columbus, Ohio]", R & D Magazine, year 2007, the 47th annual report US R&D Funding Forecast.

5. ibid, U.S. 44th, 2004

6. Wise Nano, International Research Efforts Comparison, Retrieved from "http// wisemono.org"

7. Abdus Salam, A Noble laureate for PHYSICS 1979, "The creation, mastery and utilization of modern science is what distinguish south from the north", internet.

8. This information comes from Reference: STAT/07/6 Date: 12/01/2007, of Euro stat, the Statistical Office of the European Communities.

9. F.M. Ross Hambrecht and Jr., R&D: Innovation in Industry, AAAS Report R&D FY 2006.

10. R&D Fund, S&E Indicators 2006, Internet.

11. Source: UNESCO Institute for Statistics – 2004.

12. Source: UNESCO Institute for Statistics – 2008.

13. Peter Hoy, China is gaining ground, Published October 20, 2006.

14. Xinhua, China rises to third in research, development spending, (2003).

15. Daniel Allen, Trend: Innovation not Imitation, Internet, China ramps up investment in R & D as both national and overseas companies look to leverage an increasingly favorable climate for creativity, Technology Trends, May 4, 2007.

16. John Smith: China Beefs up Research, Nation to pass Japan, 2006, Internet.

17. Social Research Collaboration Tool for Researchers, This article contains material from the Library of Congress Country Studies, a United States government publications in the public domain.1999

18. Retrieved,from"http://en.wikipedia.org/wiki/Research_and_Development_in_Japan.

19. Categories: Economy of Japan, Science and technology in Japan

20. Wagdi Swahili, Brain Drain threatens future Arab science, June 2005, Internet.

21. Faisal Sinai, the Arab Drift into Scientific Obscurity, Arab News, 2003.

22. How the Arab Compare "http://www.meforum.org

23. Barbara Crossett, Study Warn of Stagnation in Arab Society, New York Times July 2000.

24. **Wasim Maziak** Performing your original search, Arab World spending on R &D, in Science will retrieve GLOBAL VOICES OF SCIENCE.

25. Kingdom to increase research and development spending to 2.5% of GDP; Saudi Arabia will spend over SR 32 billion ($8.6 billion) on research and development as part of its 20-year National Science and Technology Plan, *Arab News* reported 2006.

26. Dr. Ata M. Hassan, L.S. Bitar and Dr. M.K. Hamid, Development of a Pan Arab R&D Institutes and Industrial Technology.

27. Sheikh Mohammed bin Rashid Al Maktoum launches foundation to promote human development with $10 billion endowment "Mohammed Bin Rashid Al Maktoum Foundation" to develop future leaders and create knowledge-based society in the region, Jordan, May 2006; see also Loai Naomani, $10 billion…. May 21, 2007-Internet.

Chapter 4 - R&D-based techno-economical Plan Changed Nations' World Order from Underdeveloped to Developed Status

By the end of Second World War, the main issue was how to repair the great economical and political damage to many nations caused by the war. The mode in many parts of the world was changed toward improving their economy and the discard of imperialism and super nationalism, which were practiced by many European and Japanese powers in addition of being also responsible for the start of both World Wars I and II. This change in European nation's economic mode and attitude led, as early as 1957, to the founding during their Rome Summit of six western European nations, to formation of the "European Economic Common (EEC)" market. The historic step was followed by the adoption of an advance R&D-based techno- economic development model plan, as early as 1960, by many of the emerging nations of the Asia-Pacific ridge countries – South Korea, Taiwan, Hong Kong and Singapore. Their adoption of the plan allowed them to change in a few decades their nations' status from developing nations to that of a highly develop, technologically advanced ones, although some were poor, militarily controlled and war damaged. The same approach was followed later on by other nations. As already indicated, many other nations including the Arab countries, the Spanish speaking countries of the South American Continent, Africa and some countries in parts of Asia plus others failed to do the same, and were left behind, underdeveloped with little progress, non-industrialized, many remained in same conditions as they were in the past several decades.

To illustrate how the use of "An R&D-based techno-economical Plan" advanced some nations while its lack-of its use kept others with little, if any advancement. Consider for illustration the techno/economic development case and status of the Asia-Pacific ridge region nations compared to that of the Arab World countries. To simplify the discussion let us start the comparison by considering as first case the progress case of South Korea to that of lack of advancement of Arab nations. The South Korea case provides an excellent example of the progress achieved in the rest of the Asia-Pacific Ridge region's countries of Taiwan, Hong Kong, Singapore and Malaysia.

4.1 An R&D-based Techno-economic Plan changed Asia-Pacific Region from developing to Developed Status

About fifty years ago, both South Korea and the Arab countries were at the same level of technological and industrial development, even some of the Arab countries had, in this aspect, an edge over South Korea. Both, South Korea and Arab World, were classified then as developing nations. As early as 1961 (4 years after the formation of the "European Common Market" in 1957) South Korea started an industrial and technology development plan that eventually yielded astonishing, remarkable economic benefits. A series of five year development plans were introduced by the country, transforming it from an agrarian agricultural economy, to an industrial, high tech one. This accomplishment was achieved in a few   decades in spite of the country then: limited resources, refugees from the north, Korea's division between disputing North and South, in addition to their recent destructive war between the two sides; also the South Korean government then was controlled by a military junta!

During this development period, South Korea adopted a technology development plan based first on building industries based on technology transfer industrial processes, followed by implementing of an R&D-based techno-economic development plan, which constitute now an integral part of their R&D-based techno-economic high tech, industrial plan. To implement the plan, which, in a way, was to some degree an imitation of other development plans used by other advanced countries, the South Korean government established, among other steps taken to achieve their goal, the Korea Institute of Technology (KIST) with many branches, with the objective of assisting the country in implementing their R&D-based economical and industrial plan. The program was also supported by R&D work done then at the universities and later on by other privately operated R&D institutes and industries [2-5]. The initial plan emphasis was on developing an electronic industry, mainly for export purposes.

As a result of this wise, well-devised and implemented plan, now South Korea is among the developed, advanced nations with a highly advanced technology R&D-based economy. About 50 years ago, the South Korean industry was comparable to that of the poorest countries in Asia and Africa, with very low GDP and per capita income. Now, as a highly advanced society, with one among the fastest exponential growth economy in the world, they enjoy a high standard of living: per capita income in year 2007 is about $24,783 compared to less than $100 per capita in 1963 and to only $82 in year 1961, the year the plan was initiated. They now have a huge international, worldwide export market not only for electronic products but also for cars, steel, tankers, power plants, wherein they are now major builder of desalination and electrical plants in Middle East and worldwide. Their highly developed worldwide economy gave birth too to many super-corporations, such as Hyundai, Samsung, and L.G. The nation's present spending on R&D is about 3% of their GDP; this percentage is among the highest in the world and is projected by the government to rise to 5% by the year 2012 [6]. The phenomenal South Korea growth is referred to by many as the "Miracle on the Han River" [2]. (This same glorious high tech fate was not achieved by its twin country, North Korea, simply because the latter fail to adopt the same or similarly effective R&D-based economical and industrial plan).

The remaining Asia-Pacific region of Taiwan, Singapore, Malaysia and Hong Kong achieved, more or less, similar success story by the use of technology based on active R&D efforts, as was done by S. Korea. For the year 2007, Singapore' GDP (PPP) per capita was a spectacular one of $49,714/annum ranking it 5th in per capita income worldwide (see Chapter 2), as compared to $41,994, $30,126 and $24,783 for Hong Kong, Taiwan and South Korea, respectively! In 1965, Singapore was a British navy base, consisting of a small fishing Island village!! Lately both the Asiatic giants: China and India are now achieving great advancement by following, more or less, similar techno-economic approach. Now, they enjoy an annual double digit growth in their GDP growth in spite of the huge number of each region population in excess of one billion inhabitants! These efforts and their benefits are shared by two other giants: Russia and Brazil, where both powers have similar GDP growth rate. For the year 2007, the GDP (PPP) per capita for: Russia and Brazil were $14,692 and $9,695 as compared to $5,292 and $2,659 for China and India, respectively [8]. Similarly we may add, compared to South Korea of $24,783 per capita income/annum for the same year 2007, Ireland per capita income rose to a spectacular value of $43,144/annum, ranking it the 7th ranked wealthiest nations worldwide. This figure compared to it being one of the poorest countries in Europe in 1965. Now people are talking about the "Miracle of Ireland" instead of its poverty as it was then.

In all cases, the Asia-Pacific region countries (Taiwan, Singapore, Malaysia and Hong Kong) started their development plan in the same manner as was done by S. Korea, first through industrial technology transfer process, followed later on by an R&D-based technology developmental plan. All and every one of them is now actively promoting technology and working on raising investment and the annual rate expansion in R&D expenditure. The industrialization process of the Asia-Pacific region countries led to the formation of many large free enterprise companies, which now they share with the government in funding most of the R&D efforts in the country (in the ratio of about 70:30%, see later section). After a half-century of technological development, many of these countries have become highly industrialized, also a model for newly emerging countries as well as an international R&D hub [9].

These countries because of the many gained benefits are determined to continue developing technology, promote economic development through technological R&D and upgrade national competitiveness along with improving the people's living standards. Government and private sectors spare no measures or funds to move technology forward by the: expansion and integration of R&D spending; training and recruiting technological personnel talent.

To ensure steady growth and ability to compete in a highly competitive world market against huge technology developed countries the governments are determined to maintain no less than about 10 percent annual growth in its own R&D budget while they encourage both government and the private sector to invest more than their present share in R&D expenditure. The governments' goal is for national investment in R&D to reach 3 percent of total GDP soon. Some are already there and with government funding accounting for about 30 percent and private sector investment responsible for about 70 percent. Various measures are also used by the governments, including cultivating and recruiting high-tech talents with emphasis on talents who possess higher degrees as the main force in R&D. (These measures for national investment in R&D to reach 3 % of GDP and the funding by government: private sector accounting for about 30:70% of expenditure on R&D are similar to same projection made earlier by "EU" for expenditure on R&D, see Chapter 3).

To protect market for their product and to allow them to compete on par level with large world economies, they are also heavily involved in R&D product development to improve, upgrade or introduce through R&D innovation new products and markets. Many of the regions' countries are now engaged in latest of R&D activities such as nanotechnology, stem cell, digital systems, etc. Without these tremendous R&D efforts they figure that they are likely to lose their market to their very giant R&D world competitors. For further emphasis on this R&D activity within the Asia Pacific Ridge region, see earlier Chapter 3 under R&D work in China and Japan.

4.2 Lack of an R&D-based Techno-economic Plan Hindered Arab Region's Advancement

Contrary to the S. Korean and the Asia-Pacific region, China, Japan and India super- success stories, also the various advances made in Europe in U.S., Canada and elsewhere in the world, which used R&D-based techno-economic plans, the Arab five year plans were nearly void of such R&D-based techno-economic plans and a supporting common market. The negligence of these steps, during the last 6 decades, was by far the main causes of neither failing the Arabs to attain an advanced technologically nor industrialized, developed nations' status. This unfortunate situation happened, as already indicated, in spite of the large influx of wealth to the region from two sources: capital wealth generated in the past in 31% of the region's countries, especially now, from sale of oil, plus a manpower wealth created by the yearly graduation of many thousands of Arab students from local and abroad universities (see Chapter 1). This great wealth, which has been wastefully exported, if it had been properly utilized, it could have contributed immensely to greatly improving the Arab nations economic, scientific, and technological knowledge and know how as well as its neighbor and the world at large.

By all standards and measures, the Arab regions countries, rich and poor, fail to measure up to advanced even emerging nations, neither in pursuing developing their industrial status economically nor in R&D efforts. They trail all nations in R&D efforts except sub-Sahara Africa, possibly in addition to a limited number of very few countries elsewhere in the world. The surprising question raised by many concerned Arab intellectuals and other none Arabs is: "why this situation was allowed to exist when the region has both the capital and manpower wealth, plenty of raw materials that can be industrialized and a significantly great need to solve the many present stagnant shortages in the production of life-essential matters within the region, especially water and food, all accompanied and compounded with an accelerated population growth rate?" Utilizing this important R&D field, many nations - such as Japan and many others - were able to excel in producing their techno-economic industrial miracles in absence of nearly all the preset raw materials in their domain. Unlike their ancestors who way back during the Arabs Golden Age Era were able to develop knowledge and science, so why can't the present Arabs do the same? The present Arabs should be awakened, search for the stimuli that made their ancestors value knowledge, R&D and therefore progress which so far they (the present Arabs) are unable to duplicate or perform.

Admittedly, during the last six decades the Arab countries had accomplish many successful achievements in building of cities, many new fancy commercial centers promoting foreign made products (which they are unable to produce), infrastructure, health care, education (wherein the region now has over 100 universities, but their curriculum is not made fully compatible with technology development), agriculture and of course defense among many other social and other economical achievements. These achievements appear to be great and significant, but in spite of all of the above mentioned ornamental but essential achievements, it is no wonder that sixty years ago the Arab World countries were classified as non-industrialized, developing nations and continue up to this date in the same categorical developing status! Definitely, different industrial, technological and economical approaches, such as used by advanced nation's - R&D-based techno-economic plans - are required to advance and develop the Arab World technological and overall economical status. The topic is discussed in further detail in Chapter 6.

(Again and again and again, it is not too late for the Arab World and other underdeveloped regions to follow suit the same approach and learn the lesson, if they want their economy to grow, prosper resulting in an overall improvement of their people living standards, establishing peace and security of the region and economy. The Arab world countries can learn from the above great achievement "Miracle on the Han River" and other advancements made by other East Asia Pacific Ridge countries).

The present historic incident is worth reporting. During my work in U.S., heavily engaged in R&D work as a Senior R&D Scientist, my great admiration of R&D contribution to U.S. economy and technology development, led me to assume - unfortunate wrongly - that the same U.S. R&D approach could be applied with some modification and tremendous benefits to Arab region, especially, great improvement of their techno-economic status. Similar R&D approach as used then by U.S. was submitted as a proposal to 20 Arab embassies in Washington, DC. The proposal dealt with the introduction, formation and development of Pan Arab R&D Institutes Initiative, with the goals and objectives of developing the Arab region's technology, industry and overall economy [7]. The proposal covered development of many specific Pan Arab R&D Institutes in water and seawater desalination, petroleum and petrochemical as well as others in development of other region's natural resources plus several others in other fields of science and tech development; all shall lead if applied to Arab region's development and status shift to advance case replacing then their underdeveloped status. The proposal, however, was not put to active implementation, with the result that the region continues to maintain underdeveloped stats. True, presently the GDP income in oil exporting countries is high, helping them to qualify to an advanced technological and developmental status; but as agreed by many, they are continued to be considered unfortunately industrially and technologically non-developed countries [8]).

...   .

References

1. Formation of EU, Wikipedia, the free Encyclopedia.

2. Economy of South Korea, Wikipedia, the free Encyclopedia.

3. Dr. Gram R. Mitchell, Korea Strategy for Leadership in R&D, US Department of Commerce, Office of Technology policy, June 1997.

4. Korea Science and Technology, U.S Embassy Seoul February 25, 2004.

5. Korea South, the Role of Science and Technology, The Library of Congress Country Studies; CIA World Fact book.

6. R&D Spending to reach 5% of the GDP: government, Korea.net Gateway to Korea, March 20, 2008.

7. Dr. Ata M. Hassan, L.S. Bitar and Dr. M.K. Hamid, Development of a Pan Arab R&D Institutes and Industrial Technology.

8. Barbara Crossett, Study Warn of Stagnation in Arab Society, New York Times July 2000.

9. List of countries by GDP (PPP) per capita, From Wikipedia, the free encyclopedia

10. The Story of Taiwan science and technology, Wikipedia, the free Encyclopedia.

Chapter 5 - Historical and Present Development of the Two Neighbors- Arabs & European Country Regions' with and without Union

"This chapter was introduced to shed brief comparative information on "Arab World" and "European Union" regions' history, present and past status with a brief summary on their role and contribution to world technology, culture and civilization with special emphasis on their exchange of information, knowledge and knowhow with and without a union. The proposed "Arab Union" modeled on "European Union" made it essential to compare the Arab and EU during two different eras at their best unionized and worst situation without a union. Specifically, the glorious past of a united region covering and ruling an extensive huge area empire, consisting of advanced society engaged in developing knowledge and knowhow during their Arab Golden Age Era (750- 1300) is compared to their present (1945 to present) developing nations status of 20 divided, none cooperative and non-competitive countries, lacking in techno-economic development, their majority are suffering from poverty and conflicts. The high effects of the 4 Islamic principles - read, write and perform R&D - on advancing of Arab nation status during the golden Age Era is also covered in some detail in this chapter. Similarly the EU region compares the EU highly developed status post the EU formation (1957- present) to that period prior to EU establishment during the period (1800-1945) of an imperial colonizing, super nationalistic, divided states system".

"Oh, East is east, and West is west, and never the twain shall meet,

Till Earth and Sky stand   presently   at God's great Judgment Seat!"

The two neighbors , East (The Arabs world- Islam) and West (Europe- Christianity), it is their many past conflicts and wars during imperialism era, invading and conquering each other land rather than their cooperation and sharing many things in common that led Rudyard Kipling, the poet, to his above famous poetry lines.

Through out history, the two neighbors, however, cooperated, exchanging many important information and events that influenced each other culture and civilization. Some countries, now part of the Arab world (the East) are the "Cradle of Western Civilization". This is also true of religion, where Christianity, the dominant religion in the West, originated, with the other twins monotheistic religions, in the East as well as many numerous, very important other cultural, knowledge and civilization programs and cultural habits. On his part, the West (Europe) contributed similarly and greatly to the East (the Arabs): first by the introduction to what is now the Arab region of the Greek philosophy and teachings, the Roman and Byzantine civil rule and government structure. Lately during the last few centuries, the west's technological and scientific work enriched the East culture, civilizations and its knowledge in science and technology as well.

In contradiction of the above poet lines, it is now the time that both - the Arabs' East and EU's West - shall meet again and cooperate in various fields; an action that is supported by the super friendly relationship now exists between the two neighbors, especially with the disappearance of imperialism and super nationalism. The European Union can aid the Arab region in development of the proposed Arab Union, catalyzing its formation the way they did in catalyzing the information and approval of the Union of Mediterranean (UM).

The following sections (5.1 to 5.5) compare how the European and their neighbor the Arab World are now and how they were with and without unity; a unity that is/was combined with scholarship and knowledge. How the two neighbors (Arab World and European "EU" countries) can cooperate, to make it – AU - happens, for the good of the Arabs as well as their European neighbors and the world at large as they already did in jointly establishing the UM, constituting 10 Arab countries – population 221 million- and 33 European states for a total combined population of over 756 million population.

5.1 The Way the European Were (1800-1945)

Imperialism, where one nation invades, occupies and controls another nation and subjugates its population to a foreign rule goes way back in ancient history, wherein King Sargon of Akkad (ca 2334 B.C.) was the first to introduce imperialism by his invasion and conquering of the nearby separate nation of Sumer, forging it in his Mesopotamian Empire [1]. The origin of European imperialism started with the founding of Alexander the Great empire (336-323 B.C.) encompassing parts of three continents [2]. This was followed later on by the Roman Empire imperialism (509 B.C, - 476 A.D) [3], which colonized and controlled all the present countries of the Mediterranean region (north, south and east) in addition to some regions in Western Europe including parts of nowadays Great Britain. The East Roman (Byzantine) empire, a split from the Roman Empire, controlled the eastern part of the Mediterranean region and Egypt (ca 527 - 636 A.D) up to its loss to the Arab Caliphate rule (836-840) [4].

Recent European imperialism in some parts of Asia, North and South Americas and Africa, however, started with age of discoveries, starting (1492) and extended to the end of World War II (1945). Our discussion, however, is limited only to the comparison of situation in Europe before World War II, during the 19th and to mid 20th centuries period (1800 -1945). During this period, the European continent consisted of a large number of divided countries, many of which were competing for a large market by establishing colonies through their imperialism system by the occupation of large parts of Asia and all Africa (1830-1945). First Arab countries to be colonized by European were Egypt (1822) by the British, Algiers (1830) by the French and Libya by the Italian in (1912). During the European colonial era, many other Arab countries were colonized and controlled by various European powers. In 1884 the conference of western powers divided Africa among themselves, which added to their imperial empires elsewhere, mainly in parts of Asia. All colonies in the Americas with the exception of a few small ones were liberated and get their independence by the year 1830, while the American Revolution led to the colonies declaration of independence, to form U.S.A., as early as 1776. Also, it was the Monroe Doctrine (1823) -America for the American- that the U.S. intervention discouraged and, more or less, stopped the European powers from meddling in American political and sovereignty affairs.

Nearly, in all cases, the European colonies in both Asia and Africa (then) were poor; some has the raw materials which can be exported to the mother industrial colonial power or elsewhere. In spite of this, the biggest glory, however, still goes to the country that holds the biggest number and land area in the colonies. To the colonial powers this form of colonial rule was considered as the ultimate in nation's power and greatness, i.e., the British government used to brag that the sun never set on their great, vast Empire. Further complicating the situation is the super nationalism that gripped a strong hold on the population and government of the great European colonial powers. In order to maintain the colonies and the empire, the colonial powers formed various alliances as well as engaged in many wars, which were waged to settle scores of conflict with other colonial powers intruding on the colony or the empire. The latest two World Wars I and II are examples.

The last World Wars II, however, was by far the most disastrous of all wars. A total of over 67 million humans were slaughtered in addition to the destruction of many cities, villages and land in Europe and around other parts of the world. Besides this great destruction, the war also brought poverty and starvation to many people in many parts of the world including Europe, to the extent that US had to provide the Marshal's aid 1947- 1950 to revive Western and Southern Europe. Yet, major super advantage of the war, it resulted in ending the era of colonialism and the liberation of all previously occupied lands in Asia and Africa, which all EU countries now admire, support and defend. To the colonies population, the colonial era represented one of the darkest ages in European and mankind history, since it subjugated the colonies peoples and government to a foreign rule of an outside invader, depriving them of self-rule and self-government. Many liberation wars erupted in both Asian and African colonies, but it was World War II that led to the colonies liberation and independence.

5.2 The Formation of European Union, 1957 to Present

By the end of the disastrous World War II, six Western European nations (West Germany, France, Italy, Belgium, the Netherlands, and Luxembourg), which were among the world countries that suffered the most from the war, met in Rome in 1957, declaring in their Rome Treaty, the establishment of the European Economic Community (EEC). The movement eventually led to the formation of a much larger European Union (EU), now with 31 European member countries. The gradual EU member building process started first by expanding the six member EEC founders to include Denmark, Ireland, and the United Kingdom (1970-73); Greece (1980); Portugal and Spain in (1986); and East Germany as part of a united Germany (1990); Austria, Finland, and Sweden (1995). The Maastricht Treaty in 1993 established a revised structure and officially changed the EEC's name to the "European Community (EC)", a title which was eventually replaced by its present name, the European Union [6].

The Treaty of Nice (2001), a revision of earlier treaties, allowed for further EU expansion of its members to include for the first time nations of Eastern and Central Europe, wherein during the period 2001-2004 ten member countries joined the union: Hungary, Poland, Czech Republic, Slovakia, Latvia, Slovenia, Lithuania, Bulgaria, Romania, and Estonia plus the two Mediterranean islands of Cyprus, and Malta. Because of the great success achieved in developing the economy and general life conditions in EU countries including peace and security, now many other European nations are trying their best to join the union. Nations who are being considered for membership include Albania (already admitted), Bosnia, Kosovo, Herzegovina, Montenegro, and Serbia. Other official candidates are Turkey and Ukraine plus others. It is expected that Russia, which already has strong economic and trading relation with "EU", may form a stronger Russian Union or may eventually join "EU" and why not, the move is good and suitable to all!

Post the European Union establishment era (1957 to present), the EU countries performed an astonishing, marvelous miracle, changed the European Union countries' status to its present very healthy glorious, united, rich and highly progressive, developed society and were able through EU formation to overcome much greater severity problems than those presently confronting the present Arab region. By comparison prior to EU establishment era, the European countries were divided, practicing an imperial colonial and super nationalism government form, suffering from several conflicts including super nationalism, ending up with the very high destructive World Wars I and II, whose major damage was seriously harmful to the extent that it forced Europe to establish its glorious, highly progressive EU.

Besides improving the region economy and technology, the formation of the "EU" is credited for bringing peace, unity, and security now noticed in the region; the union has a great and significant effect on the development of industry and technology. The union also kept the independence and form of government of each member country as it was prior to the union formation. Any disputes that may arise are solved peacefully without having to resort to war, as was done in the past.

The formation of the "EU" led to the creation of a single market in which the freedom and movement of people, goods, services, and capital among member nations is guaranteed by law. The "EU" maintains a common trade policy, an agricultural and fishery policy, in addition to a regional development policy based on adoption and implementation of an R&D-based techno-economic plan for the union. Although the average expenditure on R&D in 2006 was about 1.84 % of "EU" GDP, the "EU" goals in Research and Development, as set by the Lisbon summit strategy, are to achieve by 2010 a R&D intensity of at least 3% for the EU as a whole, and to have two thirds of R&D expenditure financed by the business sector (for more detail see Chapter3).

The 1993 Maastricht Treaty established the legal framework for "EU", while the 2007 Lisbon Treaty amended the treaty, which was ratified in 2008. In 1999 the "EU" introduced a common currency, the Euro, to be adopted by its members, now it is adopted by 15 member states. In addition to developing rules for its foreign policy, the "EU" abolished passport control among member nations.

Indeed, it is a highly beneficial union, especially when compared to unions formed during the European colonial and to pre-war era where Europe was completely divided. The benefits spill over to cover former European colonies by gaining their freedom and independence, correcting for the unhappy situation that existed during the colonial era, also by providing aid and special privileges to old colonies and population. To the world colonies, the World War II itself constituted as already indicated, a war of liberation, since all colonies got their independence and self-rule by the end of the war or shortly thereafter. How else could they have achieved their independence without this World War II? This is especially true when many of the colonial powers start to assume and seriously think, some even believed that the colony were an integral, inseparable part of the empire without it the empire itself can not exist. Many believed that the mother ruling country should defend the empire and die fighting for it. This concept became strongly embodied in the empire strategy as it actually led to the last two World Wars I and II. The strong and harsh belief of colonial people in philosophy and greatness of colonialism made the colony's people believe that without World War II, they would not have achieved their liberty; their earlier wars of liberation were fruitless; nearly all failed to liberate the colonies.

Since the formation of "EEC" followed by that of "EU", their policy now is quite different from, and in many ways presently opposite to that (the imperialism policy) prior to this period. The EU is now in full and strong support of independence and freedom to all nations of the globe in addition of aiding the poor, less developed countries; an immediate and great benefit of the formation of this blessed "European Union". What a great surprising reversal of attitude!

The following miscellaneous "EU Statistics", which covers only 27 EU members although "EU" now has 31 admitted member states, shows how great and magnificent is the present

"European Union" [6]: Population of over 500 million citizens, languages 26, Area: 4,442,773 km2 (1,707,642 sq miles), GDP in year 2007: 14,953 billion Euros, Per Capita Income $33,482 and Coastline 41,001 miles (second only to Canada).

Those fantastic benefits and achievement already gained by EU founding and techno-economic development plan can be translated into benefits to other would-be regions of the world liable to status change from developing to a developed status by following the same R&D-based techno-economic development unity plan including a great open, free enterprise market. The decimation of information on the subject shall help to serve, to encourage, to advice and to strongly promote unity formation within other various world regions. Such aid program may be donated by "European Union" to aid other qualifying regions, to execute a "Regional Union" proposal. The EU development plan Should benefit and help many developing regions, in particular the Arab neighbor proposed AU, how to smoothly build a united, open market, peaceful and secure single AU region, implementing EU formation process, including rules, regulations, and charter. The aid program is timely and very appropriate, especially in this case of AU; to assist them in developing the necessary advanced technology to move the region forward to an advanced nation's status from its present developing one, which so far they fail to achieve the union and free enterprise open Arab market alone by themselves. The aid program can be executed also at very low cost, which shall be initiated, borne and totally funded by the Arab region with "EU" only acting as a catalyst that makes union and other things happen fast. Indeed this- EU aid to AU- was the main reason and objective that made us describe in sufficient detail the various consecutive events and steps taken during the formation of EU. This move should be of great help and considerable advantage to Arab region in forming of their proposed AU.

Recently, a Union of the Mediterranean nations ("UM") was formed, joining as members 10 Mediterranean Arab countries, present population of over 221 millions, with 33 European countries. The listing and discussion of the "UM" formation and goals at the end of this chapter, Section 5.5, is quite relevant and important subject to AU formation since it combines the united efforts of both neighbors, the EU- MU and the Arab countries.

5.3 The Arab World the Way they were (750-1300)

The formation and make up of modern Arab world countries, its route, origin and start is described in detail in Chapter 1, wherein during the third Caliphates Abbasids Dynasty or other Arab rulers (750-1258 A.D.) ruled all the land between Andalusia Spain (including Spain itself) in the west to the borders of China in the east [8-10]. Unlike their predecessors, the Umayyad Dynasty, the rule of the Abbasids did not engage in further major conquest and expansion of then an already huge Caliphates empire's land. Instead, they concentrated their efforts on actively developing the society and the very extensive huge market by the development of commerce, trade, arts, manufacturing, the government system and the overall culture, giving rise to a start of Arab/Muslim Golden Age Era civilization, which was especially keen about developing knowledge and know how. They built a new capital metropolitan city, Bagdad, in 762, which became an international city and a world center, then of commerce and trade as well as a center of learning, scholarship and enlightenment. Our discussion is limited to this Golden Age Arab Era (750- 1300).

The enlighten Abbasids dynasty Caliphates actively directed the society to seek knowledge using the four Islamic principles - **Read, Write and provide R&D work, which are detailed later in the following Section 5.3.1** - and scholarship by learning science, architect and philosophy developed by others and at the same time greatly contributing their own development of the same. This era reached its climax and **"Golden Age of Arab/Moslem civilization"** during the rule of the Great Harun Al Rashid (796-809 A.D.). Harun Al Rashid's son Al Mamun (813-833) established the famous "House of Wisdom university" (Bayt al-Hekma) in Baghdad (830) with emphasis on building knowledge in all branches of science including translation of Greek, Roman and other oriental studies" [12].

"Science became an extensive cultural understanding, undertaken by the leading intellectuals in medieval Arab/Muslim society and was practiced on a scale an unprecedented in earlier human history. Work covered a variety of scientific disciplines: astronomy, mathematics, optics, engineering and technology, medicine, the life sciences, botany and pharmacology [10]". Art and architecture and the art of writing, including decorative color and philosophy including the Arabic translation of the Greek and Roman philosophical texts [see also 8-11]. The activity in scholarship and knowledge during the enlightened period work (by citizens of the empire: Muslims, Christian and Jews) contributed greatly to the tree of knowledge, which extended through the upcoming generation of Arab and Muslim rule of the region. All wrote in Arabic, which became then an international language of science and scholarship [8-11].

A great number of scientists and scholars were created and lived during this period. Amongst the greatest scientists of the era were: Ibn Sina (Avicenna) of Bukhara, wrote his Canon Book, which became the principle medicine text book in Europe for over 500 years [13]! Ibn Rushd (Averroes), the Moorish philosopher influenced the philosophy of many Europeans [14]. Al-Khwarizmi was the first to write about algebra and gave his name "algorithm" to this area of science [15]. Abu Musa Jābir ibn Hayyān (721–815), known also by his Latinized name Geber, was a prominent Muslim polymath: a chemist (alchemist), astronomer and astrologer, engineer, geologist, philosopher, pharmacist and physician, which then characterize the scientists of the period. He is widely credited with the introduction of the experimental method in alchemy, and with the invention of numerous important processes still used in modern chemistry today, such as the syntheses of hydrochloric, sulfuric and nitric acids, distillation, and crystallization. He is "considered by many to be the father of chemistry"[16]. Other Arabic mathematicians introduced the Arabic numbers 0 to 9 used now worldwide. Arabic navigators and astronomers brought the campus from China and perfected the astrolabe. Ibn Khaldun (1332-1406) an

Arabic philosopher, historian and sociologist, is credited as the founder of the sociology science [17]. Ibn Battuta, a traveler and geographer wrote very interesting articles and books on his travels through many parts of then the known world. Many others contributed to scholarship knowledge [for more detail on Arab contribution to science and knowledge and their writing see references 8-11 and the various encyclopedias as well as the internet].

Arabic language became the language of the empire with highly developed Arabic words now used in English. Books written in Arabic or authored by Arabs or none Arab scholars were then read worldwide, there were a huge number of libraries in Cordoba, Spain. Several universities date back to this era or thereafter. They valued knowledge and for this purpose build great culture and civilization including schools, libraries and universities, which continued up to now as the world oldest continually functioning institutes, such as al-Azhar (970) in Egypt, Zaytouna in Tunisia, Al-Kairaouon, the oldest university in Morocco, etc. The "House of Wisdom" (Bayt al-Hekma) university, although was built earlier in Baghdad (830) was destroyed by the Mongol invasion of Bagdad to be rebuilt recently as a new university.

Literature was very much encouraged; with the writers writing various fiction stories such as Sinbad, Aladdin, The Arabian 1000 nights' and one night plus many others were written during this enlightened era. Poetry reached its peak, producing many of the greatest Arabic poets such as Al-Mutanabbi (915-965), and poets/ philosopher Abu al-Ala al-Ma'arri* (973-1058) and many, many others known through the Arab literature during the ages (see information in encyclopedias and internet). This great period of Arabic writing in all fields of philosophy, religion, history, literature including fiction and poetry plus many others flourished and continue to be taught presently in schools and are now researched by various Arab and none Arab scholars.

During the Abbasids Caliphates' rule there existed a continuous open market, covering a huge land area from the shores of the Atlantic west to borders of China east and from South Mediterranean Sea north to central Africa south, from borders of Russia north to northern parts of India south, extending through the northern shores of Indian Ocean all the way to south Yemen and neighboring parts of Africa. By far, these Arab empires, which ruled this open market, are by far they equal nearly double all the present Arab World land. Trade and commerce activity in the region, covered all the Abbasids, Sultanates and kingdoms lands, connecting them to all neighboring regions, through land routes- the silk road and many other caravan roads- and sea routes, such as the north Indian ocean within its shores east to India and beyond, west and east Africa. Trade extended to cover the eastern Atlantic within the shores

---

* The Jews, the Muslims and the Christians,
They've all got it wrong.
The people of the world only divide into two kinds,
One sort with brains who hold no religion,
The other with religion and no brain.
–Abu-al-Ala al-Ma'arri, 10th century Syrian philosopher, poet

of north and West Africa as well as the Mediterranean, the Red and the Gulf seas. The later three seas became more or less Arab seas, where the Arab fleet and ships were freely travelling and dominating. (The Arab and later on also the Ottomans control of the three seas forced the European to seek alternative sea routs to spice rich India and silk from the orient; some of which led to the accidental discovery of America in 1492 by Columbus).

During the Arab Islamic rule many commercial and intellectual centers were build such as Bagdad, Cairo, Al Kairouan, etc, and many others were greatly expanded such as Damascus and Aleppo in Syria, Cordoba and Granada in Spain, etc. Bagdad was built, as mentioned earlier in earlier in 762, by the Abbasids, while Cairo was built by first Caliphates as an Arab military post, later expanded and made capital to many ruling Sultanate that followed the Abbasids Dynasty rule(1000-1600). When we visited   Cordova in 1997 the information pamphlet said at the time of the Umayyad II Dynasty, the city was the largest city in the world as well as a great cultural and civilization city in Europe, with many great centers of learning. Although the city was there prior to what is known as Islamic Cordoba (Qurtuba), which was conquered by the Umayyad Caliphate and made Capital of Al-Andalusia, it was ruled by the Arab for 525 years (711-1236). This period made them then the leading economic, political and cultural center during the so-called Europe's Dark Ages. The Great Mosque, which is now a main tourist attraction of the city together with many other monuments now in Spain, is the culmination of Islamic Architecture and culture in Spain [18].

Besides the above reported information, it should be indicated that the Arab World region is credited as being the **"Cradle of Western Civilization"**. It is also the home where the 3 monotheistic religions were started. Additionally, the region had also great influence and contribution to the European Renaissance movement; by the transfer of their knowledge, science and know how to Europe together with the ancient work of Greek, Romans and the East, which they translated and preserved during this medieval ages. Prior to Renaissance movement, Europe was living in the so-called dark ages.

5.3.1 Effect of Islamic 4 Principles: "Read, <u>Write</u> and Perform <u>R &</u> <u>D</u>" on Arabs' scientific and technological   society Advancement

The angel Gabriel who told the Virgin Mary that she will have a son – Christ - delivered, in years 610-632 [8 to 10], all Islamic Qur'an messages to the prophet Mohammad in Mecca and Medina, Western Saudi Arabia. The prophet   did not know how to read nor how to write, but he was highly eloquent, extremely intelligent, a great orator as well. It is because of him, the strength and appeal of Islam message and teachings that carried his followers, lead by the Caliphates (633-1300) [10], to create a vast empire covering and ruling for many centuries very large areas of land. Islam-and culture is now a worldwide faith to more than 1.5 billions [19].

Because of Islam too, the Arabic language - the language of Qur'an - became a language of many nations, remaining the permanent official language of the Arab world people, although many other countries continue to use it in religious affairs but not as their official language. Like its two great predecessors monotheistic religions of Judaism and Christianity, Islam acknowledged there is only one god to worship, same as that of Abraham, Moses and Christ. We are not in the position nor in the process to draw a comparison between the three monotheistic religions, all are great religions; rather, here we are only to bring out the content and emphasis of the very first Surah's teaching in Islam (message in Arabic constituting one chapter in Muslim holy book, the Qur'an); its past and present effect on human life as well as its relation to the present advanced nations techno-economic plan. Discussion is limited to the effect of this very important first message on   status of the Arab-Muslim Empire and population during their "Golden Age Era", particularly their development of knowledge, science and know how.

The first Islamic message - Surah - itself was very brief, consisting of **5** precise **Ayahs** (Arabic, for a sentence in Qur'an); all very instructive, extremely relevant to the economic, human life and progress. This first message was **the first to be delivered in year 610 to the prophet ahead of all other many Islam religious teachings including those of the five obligatory pillars of Islamic prayers.** The first word in this first Islamic (Surah) message was "**read** in the name of your lord -God- who has created all that exist". Because of the high relevancy of reading to human life the word **"read"** to learn was twice repeated, both in a commanding order, in the third Ayah: **"read** and your own lord is most generous and most gracious" [20]. The following fourth equally important ayah was "he has taught human **writing by a pen**". These two important human qualities acquired by teaching, **"read and write"** are complimented and completed by an equally important acquired human quality the fifth ayah "**he —God- has taught human that which he knew not"** [20]; meaning that through human hard work searching for knowledge to establish and build new know-how, a process now known as **research and development (R&D);** he God taught human the new knowledge and know-how that he did not know prior to human search efforts. Accordingly, R&D work was very much essential human quality and trait and hence highly required and extremely emphasized in this Ayah. This led us to conclude that the fifth Ayah – sentence - in Islam is the **R&D** sentence.

The above 4 Islamic principles' were also enforced by the following: ijtihad, the emphasis of both Qur'an and prophet's Hadeath on use of science and knowledge. The Arabic word ijtihad was introduced in Islam to deal with all important facts not covered in Qur'an or by Hadeath (profit's sayings, preaching and instructions). The ijtihad process means in Arabic a persistent search and learn process in order to learn, know, issue, rule, introduce law and consequently act and build. This ijtihad process constitutes an integral, inseparable R&D part of Islamic culture and law [8-10]. It further covers all aspects of what is new in human life, whether concerning religious laws (again, not stated in Qur'an or Hadeath) or otherwise new innovative and learning issues, such as the R&D work for the development of technology and other aspects of economy, social, political, etc, all relevant but in many cases unknown to human life. The ijtihad process is an extremely important one in Islam, for which many schools are and were built through out Islamic world. Many classical books are written on the subject.

Islam's concern with pursue of knowledge, scientific and otherwise was highly emphasized also in other numerous Qur'an messages, in huge number of Hadeath aided by the ijtihad process. Three Hadeath examples suffice to illustrate emphasis and role of technology in Islam: one Hadeath was "Seek science even if it was in China"; second Hadeath was "The ink of scholars is more precious than the blood of martyrs [1]", while third Hadeath said "Seek science from birth to death". The second and third Hadeath are self explanatory. The first Hadeath requests and instructs a person to seek science even if it was in China; during that time -14 centuries ago - China was considered the furthest land from Arabia. The request and teaching were made because scientific knowledge as already stated are extremely important to humans to learn, to know and consequently to invent and build.

The first Islamic message although apparently consist of only four simple words- **<u>read, write and perform R & D</u>**- its effect, when fully integrated in a plan of action with a well defined goal has a far reaching effect on human scientific and techno-economic life; equally producing the various miracles of our modern life and many other aspects of it as well. The 4 Ayahs were extensively followed by the Abbasside Caliphate during their ruling period (750-1258 A.D.), producing then many Arab-Muslim Christian and Jewish scientists, writers, poets, philosophers (see earlier Section 5.3). The Arab empire then extended from Spain in the west to the borders of China in the east was a united region, ruling on an extensive huge area of land and population; consisting of advanced society engaged in developing knowledge, scholarship and knows how. They were major contributors then to knowledge, science; advancing their society and world contributors [8-10, also see internet, encyclopedia and the many books written on Medieval Arab history]. The question is how this great difference had risen between the Arabs of the glorious past and the present era' Arabs; where by comparison the Arabs of the Golden Age era led the nations of the world in development, advancement and knowledge, while their present offspring's generation nearly trail them all – nations - in industrialization and development, with the exception of only very few nations in sub-Saharan Africa and limited number in Asia. They are now incapable of contributing knowledge neither to themselves nor to the world as was done by the Abbasside Caliphate society during their ruling period (see following Section 5.4).

Mainly because Islam (like Christianity) believes and advocates his principles and teachings universally to every human and all population worldwide, the process itself - use of this first Islamic Qur'an four very important principles - are also **<u>universal</u>** in nature. The early Muslim missionary message was the teaching of each new Muslim convert how to read, initially the Qur'an, the Muslim holy book. The process eventually lead to the start of Madrasa (school in Arabic), intended to teach reading the Qur'an which eventually evolved into teaching reading and writing to all subjects, religious and otherwise. During the "Golden Age Arab Era", the Madrasa start and building throughout the Arab Empire's land was highly progressed (for more see earlier Section 5.3); finally evolved into formation of the many universities in the Muslim world [3-5]. These university teachings were not limited to Qur'an teachings, all subjects were taught, including science, history, philosophy, social and scientific sciences, languages, etc. The realization and influence of the four principles - **read, write and perform R&D plus Qur'an and prophet teachings of science and knowledge and R&D Ijtihad** - became especially very effective in these schools as well as with the many scientists, philosophers, historians, etc; not all were Muslims(some were Christians others were Jews) scattered in the great Arab empire. It was this same effect and approach of seeking and searching for knowledge, Science and know-how that made the Arab-Muslim empire reach its Golden Age Era placing them then among the most powerful, knowledgeable nations [see references 1, 8-10 and the many books written on history of medieval Arabs; also see more detail in various development and innovative work contribution by the Arabs, especially "The Oxford History of Islam"[8] which shows in Chapter2 their contribution to: Fruit of the Tree of Knowledge, pages 62-106; while it shows respectively in Chapters 4 ,5 and 6, their contribution in Science, Medicine and Technology, pages 155-214; Art and Architecture, pages 215- 268; Philosophy and Theology, pages 269-304. More detail of Arab contribution in these fields of knowledge, technology and science are shown in Section 5.3 of this book].

Nowadays, these teachings (**read, write and perform R&D**) constitute the very important, essential approach and method to follow, by all developed nations of the world, Islamic or none Islamic nations, concerned with the development of scientific and technological knowledge as well as the nation's techno-economic and industrial plan(see the Forward book section). The R&D process now constituted an integral, inseparable part of present and past annual and long term R&D-based techno-economical plan followed now by all developed nations without any exception. How can a nation create R&D scientist without learning how to read and write, also without conducting R&D work? The result of this fixed steady approach (**read, write and perform R&D**) was the noticed great progress in developing and advancing developed nations' societies (see Section 5.3).

Unfortunately, presently the 4 Islamic principles are not used by the Muslim and the Arab countries' population for whom the first message was sent and delivered. True, some of them implemented part of the four principals, such as reading and writing, without extending the application to the other two equally important **R&D** work. Such education system results in production of high number of people who know how to read and write; but without practicing the R&D work including on-job training to learn and create, they are unable to produce new knowledgeable population. Such a system indirectly produces the adverse effect by leading to idleness and the emigration, as well known, of a large portion of them to other land already clotted with other immigrants also in search of employment. At this point we quote an Islamic Reform Scholar upon his visit to the West "in Europe I found Islam but no Muslims" reversing the saying when he came back to his home country Egypt "I find Muslims but no Islam";

meaning that in Europe they follow the above 4 basic messages **(read, write and perform R&D)** but not in the developing East, Egypt [21].

Accordingly, it can be concluded that their failure (especially the Muslims, Arabs and others) and backwardness cannot be attributed to Islam religion effect or teaching as very wrongly mentioned by many writers including many Arab writers. The claim is in contradiction of the true case of Arab Golden Age era, encouraging and sponsoring of science and development of knowledge [8-10, 28]. In the same fashion also the dark medieval ages in Europe cannot be attributed to nor blamed on Europe Christian religious background as well; now there is great number of highly advanced, developed nations existing side by side in Christian World. In both cases, lack of advancement and progress is attributed to failure of human themselves in wrongly interpreting in certain era of the religion teachings. The true interpretation and right meaning of the religion teach us otherwise, that religions do not stand in the way of nation's progress and knowledge. All religions advocate value of life, the well being of humans, their comfort and progress. In fact all religions including Islam made it nearly mandatory that followers should perform the four very important principles - **read, write and performs R&D** - as now done by all advanced and emerging nations.

5.4 The Arab World Present Status (1945- present)

Contrary to the earlier, glorious, flourishing Arab Golden Age Era (750-1300), the present Arab world situation and status are considerably different from where they were during that past Era. The changes that occurred in the region since Arab independence and self rule are numerous, having both great positive as well as negative drastic effects on the status of the region and population. Unlike the united open Arab Golden Age Era market, the nowadays Arab region continues to be divided into 20 countries, some large others very small in area and population, with minimum of inter-Arab trade among them. The existence and success of such struggling small population Arab countries (see Chapter 1, Table 1) their prospect of improved living status is very much tied to the establishment of a total Arab Union. More than the rest of large Arab countries, they will be major beneficiary of an Arab union formation and development. Therefore, they should be equally working on forging it much more than other larger countries; particularly when according to the presently proposed Arab Union modeled on European Union, each country continue too to maintain the independence and same government's form as they were prior to the union.

According to a news economic release, 2/3 of world poorest nations with an income of less than $2/ day are Muslims population including many Arabs! We have seen in Chapter 2 the very large differences in per capita income between the oil rich and the poor Arab states' population, i.e., ratio of oil-rich to oil-poor Arab countries is 31% to 69%, while the ratio of rich to poor peoples degrades and shrinks further down, due to reasons stated earlier, to only 12%

to 88%. To add to this unpleasant situation, no major trade now exists among these countries, simply because they are not industrialized countries. The latter situation compels some of them to import up to 80% or more of their industrial needs from foreign industrial nations and not from the nearby mostly agrarian Arab countries. The region, rich and poor, continues to suffer from a serious, stagnation, unhealthy crisis, more or less the way it was for the last 6 decades: developing, non-industrial, and non-advanced relative to other advanced, developed nations of the globe. Freedom of thought and decision are very much limited and curtailed, influenced by local and geopolitical and economical world affairs.

Details of other major factors and obstacles interfered in previous regional unity, Arab common market and "Arab Union" formation is listed in some details in Chapter 6, Section 6.3. Briefly these are:

- Perhaps major critical obstacles crippling the Arab region economy, hindering the Arab World progress, are the lack of use of the proper advanced techno-economic plan and the very low, insignificant R&D efforts.

- An added dilemma is the spectacular surge in oil prices, sometimes in year 2008 in excess of $145/barrel, with double edge sword effect on the regions' population. This case although gets the oil-rich Arabs -31%- richer in per capita income, on the other hand it gets the rest- 69%- of Arab population poorer. The poverty is further exaggerated in absence of aid and cooperation of oil-rich and poor Arabs.

- The shortage in production of life essential substances within the region; such as water and food production [21, constitutes another problem to Arabs' population, especially for the poor segments. They, the poor, are already suffering and highly stressed from severe and hard existing poverty problems.

- Again, the lack of strong regional stance in the face of present and future dominating world powers imposes on the region its present dominance by those foreign powers. (Principally, because of lack of regional unity, the role and say of the Arab region was frequently overlooked, many times totally ignored and their objections were completely overruled and ignored; in many cases resulting in the many conflicts and wars now characterizing the region).

- One major stagnant problem that led to severe poverty is the region's relatively very high unemployment problem. The situation forces many of its population including potentially skilled scientists to migrate- that is if allowed- to other advanced countries. The export of such manpower along with oil capital made the region number one exporter of both to advanced nations.

- Another problem degrading the Arab economy is the lack of local- from oil-rich Arabs- or foreign enterprise company's investment in the Arab region, especially the poor one.

- Still a contributing major factor to the unimpressive Arab economy is the many army revolutions (1950-1980), which occurred in the region to over through then the ruling government and supposedly improve country status. Although, they nearly disappeared from the region- mainly by the strengthens of loyal army segment to the ruler's grip on government- but the oil-rich Arab investment within the region continues to be highly and negatively effected and largely influenced by those early army revolutions. Oil-rich Arab countries continued to prefer their excess capital's fund investment outside rather than inside the region, even when recently (2008-2009) they suffered- because of present economic crises- great spectacular investment loss.

- Presently, because of lack of industry in the region, the Arab World exports and looses a large portion of its wealth (capital and manpower) to developed countries [19, 20].

In spite of these problems, recent years have seen - what considered being - a significant economic growth in the Arab World; due to rise in price of oil and the efforts by some states to some how diversifying their economic base and the many achievements that were gained by the region (for more discussion on the same subject see Chapter 4, Section 4.2). Industrial production has risen, especially in significant production of petroleum and petrochemical products. Steel production more than doubled between 2004 and 2005 from 8.4 to 19 million tones [32]. But in spite of all this, the progress in the Arab World region still of limited nature; all the Arab nations continue to be classified as developing nations, having the minimum of technology to industrialize. The Arab countries fail to do what other advanced and emerging nations have done to acquire their advanced status. Neither car making nor high tech industries now exist in the Arab World. Nearly all industrial made goods such as cars, electronic products, high tech products, armament, plus many others are imported. The Arab States continue to be - most of them - agrarian in nature, with the largest segment of the population dependent on their living on agriculture. Only a small segment, especially in oil-rich countries, derive their income from sale of exported oil, gas, refined products and petrochemical, investment or the sale of other raw materials such as phosphate. To make things worst, the region lacks the overall peace and stability necessary for economic development; many parts of the region having unrest, and some have already damaging wars such as in Iraq, Palestine, Lebanon, Sudan and many others with major disturbance and terror problems.

In many instances many Arab people tend to blame the ex-imperial European and the West for their present division and lack of progress, although very strong friendly relation now exist among the Arab World countries and the ex-colonial European nations that ruled them during the 19th and 20th centuries. They continue to claim the same failure in running their affairs on colonialism even after over 50-60 years of self rule and independence from that imperial rule! They, the Arabs, should blame only themselves for their present non-economically and non-technically progressive society. Many other nations, such as South Korea, China, India and many others suffer the same fate but they were able to overcome their so-called unhappy past, joining other advanced nations in advancing, raising their living standard, industry and overall status to that of emerging advanced societies, by following as mentioned the right, correct approach of advanced nations techno-economic plans, which the Arabs as repeatedly indicated failed to do (for more detail see Chapter 4).

To remedy their past and present sad techno-economic situation, in the past, Several Pan-Arabism movements were started as far back as 1945, immediately following independence. The movements   sought to unite all Arabic-speaking countries into one common economic market combining the entire Arab region- first total Arab common market was proposed in year 1953. Unfortunately, this total common economic Arab market was not achieved. Even total regional developmental agreement, cooperation and coordination's among the countries' region, although frequently suggested and some times proposed, very few of them were put to work and did not materialize. Furthermore, in certain critical circumstances, the region unfortunately failed to solve petty disputes and minor conflicts among the regions' governments and countries; some of which effectively ended in destructive wars among the various disputing local Arab governments. Worst yet, wars were involved with some outside foreign governments. The present Iraqi war, the Iraqi-Iran war, the Iraqi- Kuwait plus the several Arab-Israeli wars are examples (see Introduction and Chapter 5, Section 5.4).

Although total one common economic market was not realized, however, some regional Arab unions, although very small compared to the sought total Arab union, were formed. Besides the formation of the "League of Arab States" and the recently founded the "Union of Mediterranean nations"- see chapter 5, Section 5.5- only three additional regional Arab unions were formed: the short lived (1958-1961) United Arab Republic (UAR) [34], Gulf Cooperation Council (GCC) and the Union of the Arab Maghreb (UAM). These last two unions, however, failed over the past many years to reach the Arab masses ultimate goal of total common market and "Arab Union".

The Gulf Cooperation Council, comprising 6 Gulf States (Saudi Arabia, Kuwait, Bahrain, Qatar, United Arab Emirate and Oman, nearly all oil producers, total population about 39 million including about one fourth and in some small countries higher ratio of noncitizens foreign labor), was founded (1980) [35], while the Union of the Arab Maghreb (UAM) [36], modeled after ECC now EU, comprising 5 Maghreb North African States (Mauritania, Morocco, Algiers, Tunisia and Libya, two of which major producers of oil, total population about 86 million) was founded (1989). The two unions are mostly intended for some economic purpose.

The GCC achievement was in financial and monetary matters, including plans to establish a common currency in the part of the Gulf Arab region. Recently members made the decision to have single common "GCC" market by the year 2010. Each GCC member country, however, is an oil and oil derivative product exporter and is not an industrialized country; each is an importer of nearly all its commercial and life essential matter from outside the region, minimizing local GCC regional trade and interaction with other GCC countries. Furthermore, GCC's total market is very small, dwarfed by several folds in comparison to the proposed total Arab unity- AU formation as described in the proposal- or the huge EU markets; or even by comparison to the standards of any one single member country of the "European Union", such as Germany, France, United Kingdom. Each one of these last three industrial Western European countries population and marketwise is many times the size of GCC market. All these European Union countries were compelled on basis of large world economy markets to be part of the very large "European Union" open free enterprise community market.

(Would the Arabs consider the wise decision of each of these great European countries in pursuing their common market unity decision; would they also consider U.S decision that waged the Civil War in order to maintain the great unity and the free open enterprise market? For more detail on GCC's and other Arab unions, wealth and market size in comparison to that of advanced or emerging nations/regions, see Chapter 2, Tables 3 and 4. The comparison clearly indicates the minute size of Arab region market compared to those of advanced regions large world markets).

The "UAM", since its foundation in 1989, had only very few summit meetings and is significantly lacking GCC in achievement! Compared to EU great performance, UAM performance is a complete failure. The UAM most significant accomplishment was the establishment of a 7000 km highway crossing North Africa from Mauritania to Libya's border with Egypt, which could have been accomplished even without UAM's involvement. The central stretch of the highway is expected to be completed in 2010, joining Morocco, Algeria and Tunisia.

In spite of all above earlier, failed attempt for total "Arab unity", many of the final declarations and recommendations of Arab League Summits, as already indicated, still continue to recommend and call for Arab unity; specifically recommending the long waited for "the total Arab countries common, open free enterprise trade market". The last reminder was made during the last Doha Qatar Arab Summit, 2009 (for more detail on the subject see Introduction Section), but again like its many predecessor past recommendation was to no avail. The remedy and forming strategy of the region's techno-economic plan is significantly important - as emphasized through out the text - to revive and develop the region technical and industrial developmental, which should be soon implemented if the region wants improvement and significant progress (see Chapters 2-4, for more detail, see Arabic text of Summit's recommendation [26]).

At this juncture, one question regarding the investment of recently acquired Arab region's wealth- from sale of oil and huge university graduate- must be obviously raised and seriously questioned. The question constitutes an integral essential part of this important section as it constituted one in special detail in Chapter 2, Section 2.1. ***"Would it - the Arab wealth- be used unwisely invested as it was done in the past, leaving the region non-industrialized and divided, non-coordinated, suffering from many conflicts without the freedom of thought and decision as is the case now, always under the dominance of mighty nations and geopolitical and economic conditions? Or, should it be utilized wisely as proposed*** *throughout the proposal and the text, accelerating the formation of the proposed "Arab Union", developing the R&D-based techno-economic plan to bring the Arab World region to advanced (developed) nations status: provide it the prestige, the freedom of thought and free decision, make the region's masters of their destiny and decision and having the ability to contribute to science and knowledge as their ancestors did during their Golden Age era?"*

This same issue was heavily discussed during several occasions: under pressure of the first Gulf War, the then the President of U.S. and other western powers, requested that the rich Gulf Arabs share generously in aid and investment in poor Arab countries. This type of aid was practiced by the European Union where the rich Western European provided financial and technical aid to Southern and East European countries. Recently (2009), the rich EU member country leaders approved increasing bailout aid to Eastern European EU ex-communist members up to 100 billion euro. The situation- rich Arabs aid to poor Arab countries- continues to hold but with much higher urgency now than it ever was in the past; mainly because of the grave region's economic deterioration: unemployment and poverty are definitely on the rise especially throughout most of the greatly expanding Arab poor region.

In view of all the above, it can be firmly concluded that presently the Arab region gloomy and stressed case of economy calls for: a speedy immediate corrective solutions by the introduction of a massive techno-economic plan, coupled with intensive R&D efforts as well as an action to stop the region from deteriorating further into ambiguity, conflicts and worsening of techno-economic conditions. Such a plan can be achieved, as proposed earlier only through the formation of an "Arab Union" specifically modeled on European Union. The ultimate goal of the plan, its benefit outcome to the region and its rigid adherence to EU formation, objectives and implementation are justifiable and are described in detail (see Chapter 6 and Summary Section). Urgency and immediate implementation of such plan are enhanced by the soon doubling in population number: to over 600 millions by the year 2025, accompanied with severe shortages in regional water and food production as well as several other industrial and developmental shortages.

Definitely, the oil-rich Arabs can afford to fund - without harm- and jump starts the proposed AU formation and development. The task is facilitated by the openness of world markets to buy all the additional necessary technical mission requirements from equipments and needed expert local and foreign manpower. Over all, the whole region, both oil rich and poor countries, shall benefit greatly from the proposed "**Arab Union**" formation and development. The establishment of **"AU"** shall secure flow of oil from the region to the world markets and increase world trade intensity with the region and world's markets. This move will also provide- as mentioned -the region an alternative source of income providing them the power to offset volatility in price of oil and other raw materials commodities. (**Where there is a well there is way**).

5.5 The Union of the Mediterranean (UM)

The listing of the subject in this section is quite important to AU formation. The outcome of the "UM" formation is of high relevancy to our topic, it could become ("UM-EU), if properly cultivated, the catalyst greatly activating, promoting and technically aid the proposed "Arab Union" initiation, formation and development , by combining the united efforts of both neighbors- UA and Arab countries. In addition, their cooperation provides more amicable relationships and solution to common issues and problems concerning the two now very friendly regions. Further more, with the Arab Mediterranean nation's approval of UM goals, which call for the promotion and development of common R&D work among the Mediterranean Countries, the benefits gained could be naturally extended to cover the rest of Arab World. By the way, presently EU countries maintain superb, excellent relations with GCC countries as well as with UM community.

The concern of European neighbors and friends for lack of Arab world progress, cooperation, also their involvement in many of the Arab region's problems and particularly their efforts for advancing of the Mediterranean region which they share with 10 Arab states as well as also to prevent the large flow of Arab immigrants to Europe, led the French president, Sarkozy, during his presidency nomination, to re-propose the initiation and formation of the "The Union of the Mediterranean" nations. The UM was originally inspired by the Barcelona 1995 "EU" Summit meeting. Lately, after a joint, quick summit meeting in Paris (August, 2008) of European countries and Mediterranean Arab nations, both parties quickly approved the initiative, electing both France and Egypt representative' presidents to head "UM" for the following 2 years. A permanent secretariat will be established later [22-23].

The "UM" historic founding was made with the objectives of a political, economic and a cultural union among the European side (all "EU" members) plus Balkan States that are not "EU" members and the Arab Mediterranean nations, for a total of 43 member nations, with the "UM" becoming a home to 756 million people from the shores of Greenland to the Jordan desert. "The "UM" establishment shall do the same things with the same goal and same method as "EU" but will not be based on "EU" model nor shall it be a complete union with EU [22]"!

During the summit, they agreed on a batch of modest projects: "environmental protection in the Mediterranean, development of solar energy and water management, solutions to increase natural hazards and infrastructure, and the transport deficits, economic and social developed programs and higher education and research programs". The agreement, however fell short of a full union as that followed by EU, nevertheless, it is a great forward step toward full coordination and cooperation between the two parties, solving amicably of outstanding problems concerning and confronting the two parties.

Most of the Arab Mediterranean nation's head of states or their high representatives attended the Paris Summit although surprisingly many heads of Arab countries fail earlier, mainly because of region's sensitivity to outside geopolitical reasons, to attend the "Arab League" meeting held in year 2008 in Damascus. Two head of states- Egypt and Yemen- also did not attend the more recent 2009 Doha Arab Summit! The quick response of heads of Arab Mediterranean countries, which represent a majority of Arab population (about 221 million out of total of over 329 million), attended the meeting, made no surprise to many observers; evidently they, the Arabs, were looking forward for such union to succeed, achieving the "UM" goals. Although it is premature to rule-out on the success of the "UM" initiative, the question remains why the "UM" initiative was accepted while the many other Arab World meetings, many calling previously for Arab Union failed?

The summit meeting was attended by the Arab Mediterranean nations head of states also in spite of Israeli attendance; although their summit joint meeting with Israeli representatives was a taboo case, nearly forbidden in most other past meetings outside the UN. The attendance of many heads of Arab States and their initial fast approval of "UM", compared to the failure of many others- Arab head of states to attend the earlier Arab League in previous meetings, showed the great relevancy of UM to the Arab region and more so enforced the assumption that at last the Arabs who attended the Paris Summit meeting are tentatively in support of Union formation even with their neighbors. Presumably, the Arabs, considered such union of major advantage and of great benefit to the revival and improvement of the saddened case of these Arab' nations economy and population. Additionally, it too established a   stronger needed communication and cooperation with an obviously friendly, highly advanced neighbor, with both the European and the Arab Mediterranean states sides gaining great benefit from the union.

In view of the earlier failure of the Arab to reach a unity compared to the apparent success of the Paris Summit meeting process suggests that: the European must have catalyzed   the "UM" initiation and formation. Definitely the European faction seems to have the "magic lamp" touch in making unions happen, a move that Arab region was not able to accomplish it alone by themselves. Because of their- EU- great ease in getting UM's approval; a suggestion was made: why not asks EU to assume the responsibility of approaching the Arabs to start and develop the proposed Arab Union? This question can be raised by the "UM" Arab members who possibly can cultivate UM/EU to perform this magical task in the same speedy manor as they did in establishment and approval of UM.

...   .

References

1. King Sargin of Akkad…, Patricia S. Daniel and Stephen G. Hyslop, Almanac of World History, Library of Congress Publication, 2003.

2. ibid, Alexander the Great, pages 55, 89, 94-95.

3. ibid, The Roman, pages 80-85.

4. ibid, The Byzantine, pages 102,110-113.

5. ibid, Age of DISCOVERY, 174, 180-191.

6. R&D in EU, http://europa.eu/rapid/press Releases Action, reference=STAT/07/6, 12, Jan., 2007.

7. Jean Monnet, "The European Union as a Model for Regional Integration: The Muslim World and Beyond," Jean Monnet/Robert Schuman Paper Series Vol.6 No.1 January 2006.

8. Oxford History of Islam, Editor John L. Esposito, Oxford University press, 749 pages, with 15 contributors, 1999.

9. ibid, by Fred M. Donner, Muhammad and the Caliphate, pages 1-61, Chapter 1, Political History of the Islamic Empire up to the Mongol Conquest.

10. ibid, by Vincent J. Cornell, pages 61-106, Chapter 2, Fruit of the Tree of Knowledge.

11. ibid, Chapters 3-5 pages 107- 269, written by various contributors on: law and Society, Science Medicine & Technology, ART& Architect and Philosophy & Theology, respectively. Other chapters pages 270-710 by numerous contributors about other Islamic affairs, countries, culture, empires, etc.

12. ibid, Al- Mamun, Abbasid Caliph who built the House of Wisdom –knowledge in Bagdad, pages 272, 331 and 693.

13. ibid, Ibn Sina (Avicenna), pages 170,181, 204-205.

14. ibid, Ibn Rushd (Averros), pages 175,286-289.

15. ibid, Al-Khawarzmi, pages 157, 184-188.

16. ibid Jabir ibn Hayyan, page 198.

17. Ibid, Ibn Khaldun, pages 291-293.

18. Cordoba, from Wikipedia, the Free Encyclopedia.

19. Major Religion of the World Ranked by size and number of Adherents, www.google.com/search.

20. Interpretation of the Meaning of the Noble Qur'an in the English language, Surah96, pages 779, Maktaba Marrussalam 1994, Muhammad Tagi-U-Din Al-Hilali and Dr. Mohammed Muhsin Khan, 1994.

21. **Wasim Maizak, Performing** your original search, Arab World spending on R &D, in Science will retrieve GLOBAL VOICES OF SCIENCE.

22. Wagdi Swahili, Brain drain threatens future of Arab science, June 2004, Source: SciDev. Net.

23. Immigration to EUROPE, from Wikipedia, the Free Encyclopedia.

24. Ata M. Hassan, the Blue Revolution, San Diego, California, U.S.A., 2006.

25. European Union from Wikipedia, the Free Encyclopedia.

26. The Union of the Mediterranean (UM) countries from Wikipedia, the Free Encyclopedia.

27. The United Nations Development Program (UNDP) released the Arab Human Development Report 2002, july 2002.

28. *Nature* **444**, 35-36 (2 November 2006): 10.1038/444035, Islam and science: Where are the new patrons of science?

29. Arabic text of Arab League Summit Meeting Recommendation, Doha, Qatar, March 2009.

Chapter 6 - Proposed Formation of an Arab Union Specifically Modeled on European Union Awakens and Advances the Arab World Region from Underdeveloped to Developed Status society

"By the end of the World War II (1945), drastic changes occurred in world political and economic order. The world nations' concept of old style colonialism and super nationalism, which were practiced prior to the war by both the European and Japanese's powers that also caused the disastrous wars, were completely discarded. They were replaced by a new geopolitical and economic world order granting freedom and independence to all previously colonized world nations. Great emphasis and concern were also directed on how nations can fix the already war damaged pre- and post-war *world economy. To remedy the sad economic war situation, all now world advanced nations/ regions shifted their effort toward the revival and development of their prewar and postwar techno-economic status; industrial and otherwise. This same R&D-based techno-economic approach was joined by many other already or newly independent nations such as the Pacific Ridge Countries; achieving also developed or emerging nation's status. The huge lands and massive populations of: Brazil, Russia, India and China (***BRIC*** countries' group) all are now pursuing more or less this same techno-economic advanced nations approach that yielded them the recently acquired - year 2007- high double digit growth economy. Contrary to these groups, many other nations/regions fail to pursue the same advanced nations' techno-economic trend; remaining as they were, suffering in their present non-developed status. This chapter deals with the proposal: "how to change the status of those presently developing nation/region to that of advance developed nations status by following and rigidly implementing advanced nations' techno-economic plan [1-25]". The proposal utilizes the establishment of the proposed AU specifically modeled on EU as an example, illustrating the process; also how the proposed plan - the proposal - was generalized to cover other would-be cases that are determined to make the conversion move from poor, developing to that of rich, advanced status".*

As already reported in Chapter 5, Section 5.2, Germany together with 5 other Western European countries founded the European Economic Community (EEC) market in 1957, which duplicated more or less, a similar approach of having: a U.S.-style open, free enterprise market, but utilizing union of countries instead of the U.S. states confederate model. The R&D-based techno-economic plan, which was utilized by other then advanced rich nations, such as U.S.A, became more or less the standard plan for all now advanced nations.   As reported earlier, a similar R&D-based techno-economic, educational plan was also rigidly utilized successfully by Japan and by other emerging nations, such as South Korea and many other Asia Pacific ridge region' countries, as well as by China, India, Russia and Brazil. Israel too, now part of the Arab land region, in spite of limited natural resources, is highly advanced using same developed nations' techno-economic plans. The great techno-economic accomplishments following rigid techno-economic planning of these nations qualified some of them, after many years of relentless hard work, to be presently classified among the members of the well-known G-8 world richest nations: U.S., Japan, Germany, Russia, United Kingdom, France, Canada and Italy. Although China is not included among the G-8, it is now (2009) the second richest world economy and second only to U.S.A also in R&D funding. China's latest technological, industrial and economical progress and achievement are being admired worldwide.

In contrast to these developed and emerging nations, the techno-economic effect, however, did not extend also to many nations presently all classified now as developing nations. Unfortunately the phenomenon included also all Arab World countries, although they are now constitute highly candidates to catch up with advanced nations by forming as already proposed the "AU modeled after EU". This assumption was further supported and enhanced since collectively the region possesses the means and tools to perform the task. Still very essential is that the AU formation and execution must necessarily adhere to and rigidly follow the advanced nations' techno-economic plans. Additionally, the generality applies only if the Arab region has the will and determination to collectively fully cooperate to undertake and perform the transformation job.

In the past, various movements and geopolitical and local economic conditions that prevailed during most of the past 6 decades, although resulted in the formation of EU, for some reason or another they fail or were not sufficiently adequate to create a great total Arab open common, free enterprise market nor union. Vice versa and very likely, the Arab region itself was not ready and prepared to perform the union, although many excuses were given to justify the failure.

Presently, however, the Arab region as indicated possesses all the tools and proper qualities that can allow it to induce the transformation change from developing to developed status. The move is especially urgently required in order to improve region's present and future expanding population's living standards and as well solve the many outstanding shortages and stagnant problems now confronting the disunited, uncoordinated, uncooperative region. In balance, the region also possesses many favorable local and geopolitical economical conditions and stimuli, some already mentioned in earlier sections (see Chapter 1, 5, Section 5.4 and others are being discussed in this chapter, Section 6.4). Those stimuli if utilized - and economic and political conditions say it must be applied - would accomplish the long sought progress including formation of a united great, open Arab common market. The continued unnecessary delay of such regional initiative shall keep the region in this poor status and may cause it even to regress.

The proposed "Arab Union" selectively and purposely modeled on "European Union", rigidly operated on the up-to-date EU's and other advanced nations industrial R&D-based techno-economic plan, is by far the most adequate applicable plan that shall guarantee development of an advanced Arab region and common market. The present abundant regional and international stimuli are more than sufficient to convince all Arab countries' government, strongly forced and supported by the massive population, to initiate a fresh and serious approach toward the formation, implementation and completion of an Arab Union - with EU aid and assistance. There is no better strategy and plan that can better compete with this proposed AU initiative. The plan as indicated is anticipated to provide the region with numerous benefits to all: rich and poor, present and future generations, both governed and governed Arabs segments. The AU formation shall also benefit European and world's population as well. The remaining parts of this chapter describes how the proposed accomplishment- formation and development of "Arab Union" specifically modeled on "European Union"- can be achieved; the various factors that interfered with the union formation and others that presently promote and stimulate it, as well as the many benefits gained by AU establishment and development for both the Arab and European regions and the world at large.

6.1 "European Union" a super model to "Arab Union"

It was assumed through out the previous chapters that the implementation of "Arab Union" Modeled on "European Union" Changes the Arab World's Industrial Techno-economic Status. A big endorsement of this EU choice can be found in the continued great eagerness and enthusiasms of the many European, and none European countries, who are anxiously and impatiently waiting to join EU membership, such as Turkey and Ukraine. In this section, a brief summary of "why EU was selected as an AU super model" is presented, which is further supported in following sections 6.2 by other writers [3, 4-7] as well as by the many favorable conditions and stimuli listed in Section 6.4:

First, and foremost the establishment of the proposed AU shall create a huge area of land and population common Arab region's market. The market success, however, requires a selection of an equally huge region, techno-economically successfully proven model. Definitely, the undisputable striking techno-economical and immeasurable political successes of "EU" countries more than qualify it to be the chosen super model. All the already acquired EU benefits shall be also acquired by the Arab countries upon AU appropriate, complete implementation. Such great benefits are summarized   in the book's "Summary Section". Briefly, the establishment of AU shall create stability and improved Arab economy and employment within the region as well as brings great benefit also to EU by: minimizing Arab manpower immigration to EU, improved trade and flow of goods between the two parties, including oil and gas flow from Arab world to EU countries. In addition, greater cooperation and coordination between the two regions shall be amicably pursued and maintained, with mutual benefit to all.   The magnitude of such anticipated shared benefits should stimulate EU not only to enhance but also to aid the Arab side in the formation and implementation of the proposed Arab Union!

Second, according to the "EU" model, each new Arab member country within the union - AU - retains his present independence status and same form of government without change; a great unity stimulating, promoting factor; the earlier overlooking of which caused many earlier Arab conflicts, and wars; preventing earlier Arab past unity attempts to materialize. The factor is as it was of great and considerable, critical interest to all past and present Arab countries governments' and rulers without exception; since as it is well known fact that many Arab governments and rulers are keen and will not give-up the country's rule nor independence or type of present government. The situation tends to be a legitimately inheritance right case of father-to-son (so far no daughter has ruled an Arab country, although they ruled other Islamic countries). In the past many battles and wars were waged to preserve and maintain the now existing form of government. The above factor constitutes core of an important factor that in the past not only hindered Arab unity (see following Section 6.3) but equally led to the first Gulf War when Iraq invaded Kuwait. The war, as well known, ended when foreign powers led by U.S.A freed Kuwait. In a way, the war was followed later on by the present Second Gulf War and the temporary U.S.A's occupation of Iraq.

(***Presently***, *however, an "AU" selectively modeled on EU, enforces this more or less sacred rule - maintenance of independence and form of present government - since it allows and totally, fully supports the concept, as now done at EU, without neither disturbing nor violating it*).

Third, the AU modeled on EU creates a regional unity as that now exist in EU region, which provided the EU region the extremely important, geopolitical and economic strong stance in the face of the many present and future dominating world powers. In the same fashion, the creation of AU guaranteed the same privilege to Arab region, providing it too the strong stance in face of dominating foreign powers. This anticipated acquired stance compares to the present weak one, where in many present occasions, because of lack of regional unity, the role and say of the Arab region was overlooked, many times totally ignored. The creation of AU shall create unity, prosperity and too stop invasion of Arab land by those dominating world powers as was done lately by U.S.A's occupation of Iraq.

Fourth, another important factors that calls for EU selection as AU model is the proximity, neighborhoods of the two Arab and European regions; their joint sharing of markets, history, civilization, involvement, influence and the continuous interference through the ages in each other's affairs and policies support the choice. Unlike the previous era wherein the two regions were fighting each others, each region occupying parts of other people's land and by the end of European imperialism, the two neighbors are now enjoying best of friendly relationship, which again strongly support the EU model selection. Many presently favorable geopolitical and economic factors are now leading to greater cooperation and coordination between the two neighbors as most recently demonstrated by the joint formation of the "Union of the Mediterranean" (see Chapter 5, Section 5.5) and the Euro-Arab dialogue to which the author contributed the proposal for the joint development of an Arab R&D Water Resources and Desalination Institute.

Fifth, the many above convincing stimulating factors are being further supported, emphasized by the fact that prior to the last World War II, the European community was facing much more serious problems than those problems presently facing and characterizing the Arab world. They - the Europeans - were able to overcome them by the EU formation. The way EU solved these previous problems can also help AU solve the many outstanding problems presently confronting the Arab region through the establishment of AU and the anticipated EU aid program. That is if the Arab world can learn this extremely good lesson; knowing the type and nature of these problems and how the Europeans were able to overcome them. Definitely, this case constitutes a significant stimulus to the Arab region governments and private sector to logically argue the great benefits gained by EU formation and how the same gain can be extended to the Arab side by the implementation of AU modeled on EU. The many wars that came ahead of the EU establishment made the European come to their senses, correctly thinking and arguing to quit that unfortunate old previous political imperialistic and super nationalistic concept, replacing it by the formation of their present glorious EU unity and the establishment of a common, giant open free enterprise market and system.

(But, would the Arab learn and absorb the lesson by duplicating the act, forming AU or continue to claim they are doing the same unity by having their GCC, UAM and UM which all fail so far to raise Arab status from where it is now- completely underdeveloped-to a higher developed status?)

<u>Sixth,</u> one important reason for the selection of EU model case is the special good, friendly relations that now exist between many of the Arab countries and their ex-European colonial powers. Many Arab countries were up to 1945 conquered and ruled then by many of the imperialist European nations, now all members of "EU". In most cases the Arab countries inherited and were very much influenced by the imperial European governments rule, including schooling system, language use, to some extent tendency to follow same EU governmental structure and operation, plus gaining knowledge and custom of doing many other things the European way. Special relations continue to exist between the two parties, the previous European imperial power and its previous colonized Arab country, such as the special relations now exist between France and North African counties, France and Lebanon, Great Briton and U.A.E, Jordan plus other Gulf countries. The imperial rule also contributed to the Arab World partition and division into 20 countries and now time for "EU" to correct

the situation by helping the region in building region's unity by aiding the Arabs in the establishment and catalysis of the proposed "Arab Union"- the same way EU catalyzed UM formation. All these set of issues and facts made it obligatory that these ex-colonial European nations, now EU members help their previous Arab colonies develop themselves – forming AU - as now was done through European Union formation.

(**But** *also, would the Arab region's countries cultivate these special, friendly relations by seeking EU aid and help in establishment and development of AU modeled on EU? But if they fail all governments and private sector they shall suffer*).

Seventh, still there are more compelling reasons for EU being the super model selection to AU. Through the ages: ancient, medieval and present eras, there were considerable exchange of information and culture between the two neighbors. "**The development of western civilization**" is credited to start in countries that are now part of the Arab world. **Christianity** came to the West from the East, now part of the Arab countries. The Arab region's knowledge developed during the medieval ages together with ancient knowledge they translated from ancient Greeks, Romans and others, which they preserved, contributed significantly to the European enlightenment movement (**Renaissance**) of the very late middle ages. On the other hand, the West (Europe) contributed similarly and greatly to the Arabs: first by the introduction of the **Greek philosophy and teachings, the Roman and Byzantine civil work** and culture as well as lately during the modern ages the European did their big share by contributed significantly to the **world knowledge**, including that to the Arab World population by the advancement they achieved in many fields of **science, technology and civilizations** (for more detail see Chapter 5).

(**Now** *is the time for further exchange of benefiting knowledge to continue between the two now friendly neighbors, with European Union doing the favor by presently aiding the Arab side catalyzes the formation of an "Arab Union" modeled after their very highly successful "European Union" as they already did earlier: the formation and set up of UM. Moreover, the two neighboring regions share many common features and problems; their solution has major simultaneous, mutual benefits and effect on both regions*).

At this juncture, it is wise and advantageous to briefly reemphasize that the Arab side discuss in detail with the European Union side the history and causes of previous failure attempts of union formation among the various Arab countries in comparison to the successful European Union formation; with the purpose of Arabs finding solution to overcome and completely avoid disunity problems as was achieved by EU in overcoming their much more, as already stated, severe earlier problems, that rose during World Wars I and II. Definitely, none of the past and now existing Arab region's problems is equal in severity and magnitude to European World War II immense loss and disastrous harm. Nevertheless the European was able to forget and to overcome all these very hard and difficult problems; why can't the Arabs do the same? Summaries of the these problems that interfered earlier in the formation of an "Arab Union" as well as the many present, positive, strong encouraging, geopolitical and economic and local stimuli for the formation of a proposed "Arab Union" are presented in the following two sections of this chapter, respectively; while the final Sections of the book - Sections 6.5 and 6.6 - describe respectively first a proposed process recommended for the "Arab Union" formation and second "how to enhance and greatly advance the AU's very important R&D Efforts in the region". Now, in presence of tremendous number of positive local and geopolitical and economic stimulus factors and conditions promoting the proposed Arab Union, it is time again and again for the Arab region – government and private - to seriously reconsider implementing the proposal "Arab Union" modeled on "European Union".

*(**Certainly**, as illustrated in this Chapter 6, the proposal deserves Arabs' population and government's consideration and recognition of AU formation and complete implementation, without loosing and wasting this golden opportunity, as was done during the last 6 decades; carefully studying, by the decision maker - the government - and private sector, the effect and implication of AU formation and development on advancing status of the present and that of the future Arab generations, which is doubling in number, problems and shortages as well).*

6.2 Major Work Done Related to Advance Arab Region, Improve Region's Tech and Formation of "Arab Union" modeled on "European Union"

In general, it can be stated that despite the various advances that the economies of certain countries within the Arab World region have made recently in several fields, all the countries within the region continued to be classified as developing countries. There is a unanimous agreement that the oil-rich exporting GCC Arab countries, although they accumulated great wealth and their population has high GDP per capita income, yet they continued to be classified technologically and industrially as non-developed countries [8]. The classification is supported by United Nations and developed nations' rules and indices. Principally, this situation came about as a result of the region's lack of: unity, free common enterprise market, industrialization, use and application of modern techno-economic plans. Equally contributing to this situation is the continued increase in region's population - together with an increase in peoples' cost of living - at a much higher rate than the regional economic growth rate.

No major industries based on technology transfer processes, information technology or electronic industries, nor even car factories, aviation or materials manufacturing, or other high tech industries neither exist now nor were introduced in the region. No major advancement in raising R&D efforts or funding, were made also so far. Activity in this important field continued to be very small, industrially and scientifically ineffective. This situation left only a limited number of industries in the region, which continue to depend, to a great extent, on export of raw commodities, mainly petroleum and petrochemical products, with majority of population engaged in agriculture and some in trade. The overall output of this sad situation is the noticed minimum of trade activities conducted among the various industry-lacking countries within the region; the ratio of rich to poor Arab countries' population stands now only at the very low, meager value of 12 to 88%.

Furthermore, unfortunately, neither a Pan-Arab R&D program nor cooperative coordinated Arabs' regional approach initiatives now exist among the region's countries with the objectives of developing the Arab region's technology, industry and overall economy that should lead to free open common Arab market formation. Many of the region's local and foreign problems increased. Also, aid from oil-rich to poor Arab World countries was inadequate to lead to major change. To make things worse, the major export of region's main wealth to advanced countries – capital cash and potentially scientific manpower – which for the benefit of the region should have been reversed, continued. Instead of importing skilled manpower to help them raise industrial and technological level of the countries, rather they are fully engaged in importing huge manpower number to provide, in most cases, common services that can be done by the native Arabs.

Work related to the subject, specifically how to improve political and economic status of Arab World Countries, in order to introduce an up-to-date modern Pan Arab techno-economically based economy, cooperative R&D efforts, establishment of common market and "Arab Union", were examined by numerous investigators. A study of the subject is far beyond the scope of this book. Our review, however, will be limted to several investigations related to the founding and development of the proposed Arab Union and Pan Arab R&D cooperative efforts.

One of the earliest such investigation was carried out by one of the authors. During his long and continuous R&D career working in U.S., admiring U.S.A's achievement as the richest world economy, through unity, open free market and use of a highly progressive R&D-based techno-economic plan, he jointly with other distinguished scientists submitted a joint proposal to each of the 20 Arab embassies in Washington, DC (1967). According to the proposal they - the 20 Arab countries' region - can too develop and advance their technology and economy by following U.S.A's techno-economic plan. The proposal itself then in addition to calling for the introduction and implementing many other industrial and technological steps, it called also for the establishing of numerous scientific and technological Pan Arab R&D Institutes to develop shared technology and industrial development within the region [3] (for more detail see also Chapter 4, Section 4. 1). Unfortunately, the proposal was not put to application; its negligence and lack of other industrial and economic development kept the region in its present developing status.

In this present book, Dr Hassan in cooperation with his son, an expert and developer of scientific and information technology, worked on the revival and expansion of the above 1967 proposal to all Arabs: "how to change nation/region from a developing to a developed, progressive status society; purposely awakening the Arab region to form the proposed "Arab Union" specifically modeled on "European Union". The case is used to illustrative how this

AU Initiative should help the Arab region duplicate similar EU-model's techno-economic advantages. Simply, the proposal message reveals that: "only through adoption and development of technology and R&D-based techno-economic plan, combined with a fully integrated compatible education, technological and industrial systems; rigidly implemented and routinely followed on continuous basis, that the Arab and other underdeveloped world countries are able to shift and progressively achieve a develop nation status from their presently developing one". Several cases are presented to demonstrate how, by rigidly pursuing this plan, nations and regions shifted their unhappy techno-economic, developing status to that of an advanced, high tech case (see Chapters 3 and 4).

Numerous other articles directly related to the above subject were written. One such article was written by Jean Monnet [4], which carried the title: "The European Union as a Model for Regional Integration the Muslim World and beyond", in particular he used "the European Union as a Yardstick against which the Strength of Arab Regional Integration can be measured". The article dealt directly more than the rest with the present subject - Arab Union modeled on European Union. Other articles released by the United Nations Development Program (UNDP) in an "Arab Human Development Report 2002" [5], dealt very much with related topic on the same subject. Because of the high relevancy of these two last investigations to the present proposal, they are briefly reviewed here.

The most important finding of Monnet's report [4], was that he found Among the European's members: "a wide variety of issues around which agreement and bargaining occur; a high degree of harmonization, mutual recognition of policies, and institutionalization; a degree of transfer of competencies to the Union; and a widespread feeling of a common identity and/or mutual obligations among the people of the Union". The same indicators are "only weakly present in the Arab contexts. Closer integration is hampered by the absence of a well-embedded institutional fabric, political commitment among the governments or leaders, and a transnational business culture seeking the establishment of economies of scale". The author conclude that "Arab integration therefore represents a form of integration that needs to develop more strongly along the above mentioned EU lines in order to reach a real integration potential. To promote such a development means dealing with prevailing geo-political circumstances and introducing domestic political reforms. The two are heavily interlinked". Furthermore, the author claimed that in the Arab World case "citizen participation and private sector initiative have remained constrained". The author gets support to his views by reference to views on the subject by other investigators [4].

In spite of the above analysis of the situation and the shortcoming of dialogue, coordination and collective regional work, the author remarked that "It will be interesting to see to what extent Arab states can take up this challenge and overcome differences in the economic ideological and political fields". Yet, the future development of Arab regional integration must also be seen in its relation with other Muslim's world (whether on a general or sub-regional level). "Should the Arab regional integration efforts become stronger, and more like the integrative forms of the "EU", a number of potential consequences or implications might also merit further attention". Finally, also of interest for the future, "will be whether the EU will promote greater Arab regional integration efforts, and how the "EU" will relate to these both economically and politically."

The comments and conclusions of the author - Jean Monnet [4] - **firstly** are in agreement with our correct selection of "EU" as the model for Arab to pursue in formation of an integrated Arab Union; and **secondly**, how the role of "EU" will promote and propagate greater Arab regional integration efforts; also how the EU will relate to these both economically and politically? Wherein we recommended that "EU" should act on this mission by providing their technical aid program to "AU", catalyzing the formation and implementation of the whole process, the way they catalyzed the European- Arab "Union of the Mediterranean"(UM). The European Union's aid benefits AU, which is illustrated elsewhere in this chapter, is very great and immense in advantage to both regions. Their involvement should stimulate and promote AU formation and development. We further advocate that EU should work actively on promoting the Arab Union formation and development and with the oil-rich Arabs should bear the AU's developmental cost (see Section 6.5).

Thirdly and very important, the author recognized, as we did, that the founding of AU modeled on EU's great success story in solving the many problems - the European encountered prior to "EU" formation and the fantastic benefit gained thereafter - can too uplift and advance the Arab region. He saw that "It will be interesting to see to what extent Arab states can take up this **challenge** and overcome differences in the economic (rich and poor states), ideological (Sunnis versus Shiites or fundamentalist versus moderate forms of Islam) and political (over cooperation with western states, especially the United States) fields". In fact, the challenge was taken positively, promptly and quickly by the 10 Arab Mediterranean countries. They joined the UM formation and approval, although it is made of different nations, races, languages, culture, religious sects, political, etc. The **greater challenge**, however, continues to persist: whether they, the Arabs, can satisfy the challenge - by forming the all Arab countries AU, as they positively did in implementing their 10 Arab Mediterranean countries, joining and establishment of UM. Optimistically, the same act can be followed by the rest of Arab nations in formation and development of the highly beneficial AU Initiative, specifically modeled on EU.

It can be independently argued further that the tremendous benefits and advantages already gained by the European - including avoiding disastrous wars, replacing it with peace and security; having an open great free enterprise market; free thought and decision, plus other benefits - can be also achieved by the Arabs' proposed AU's unity formation and development. The argument is further supported by the present great stimuli of vast wealth in capital, from the huge surge in oil prices and the great number of Arab graduates from home and abroad universities. This stimulus of rise in capital, which is considered here as one of the most significant stimuli in promoting AU formation, was absent in Monnet argument since his article was written prior to the great surge in the phenomenal 2008 oil prices. In turn, the previous argument also has great effect on a very important second stimulus of "how to avoid the many present and future problems and chaos associated with the certain great, expected expansion in region's Arab population to double its present number of over 329 million within the coming two decades". How the Arabs shall coup up with this vast number and their futuristic problems, remembering that the Arab region is already now suffering from acute shortages in the production of many life-essential materials as well as it is already suffering from several severe problems such as great unemployment, lack of regional development plus many others! Definitely, the situation not only can be much tolerated by the excess capital in the region but it also demands as already concluded, the immediate development of new, improved strategy and planning, which again can be met by the formation and development of AU modeled on EU; enforced by EU aid in catalysis of the AU process formation and development.

The Arab Human Development Report 2002 [5] was compiled by a "group of distinguished Arab intellectuals" led by Egyptian statistician Nader Fergany. It caries a lot of materials and discusses a great number of highly relevant issues that relates to lack of progress in the Arab world and recommendation on how to deal with them. The report itself consists of a lengthy report (168 pages) which was released on July 2, 2002, by the United Nations Development Program on the Arab Human Development case. The report has a wide review by a good number of reviewers and specialists in the Western and Arab media [6-11]. With support of a lot of statistics, the report as stated "tells a sad, sorry story of two decades of failed planning and developmental decline"; (actually the decline started with their independence, about 6 decades ago). One inescapable conclusion emerges from its sober pages of tables and charts and other disappointing statistical figures is that: "the Arab world is in decline, even relative to the developing world [5]", meaning newly developed emerging countries such as South Korea, Hong Kong, Taiwan, Singapore, China and India.

The content of this second report [5] along with the various remarks on it [6-11] are in agreement with our findings, which are further supported by the findings and views of many other reports written and related to the subject by various other writers [12-13]. All are in agreement that the Arab World countries failed to improve the region and move it to adopt and use modern industrial and R&D-based techno-economic systems as was done by developed, advanced nations. In particular, they fail to produce, a fully integrated total Arab Union, such as European's "EU" nor the essential industry and technology necessary for the region's advancement and raising of Arab population standard of living and in consequence the expansion of inter-Arab trade. Lack of regional communication and coordination of communal development programs not only contributed to the region's failure in achieving the masses' desire for unity and improved economy, but also led the region to a regress condition compared to that of other nations, which managed to advance, upgrading their status from that of under developing nation to a developed one in spite of many obstacles that confronted them including severe poverty during this remarkable transformation period.

The report and all comments on it by various writers call for greater Arab regional cooperation and coordination by: providing solution to their many problems, departure from their old economical and industrial plans and approach in country and region's development, replacing them with new modern techno-economical plans; some call for an outright formation of Arab Union. In effect, they lend a very strong support to our message for total change in the previous Arab techno-economic plan for an improved development of the region by the formation of an Arab Unity.

6.3 Summary of Major Factors and Obstacles Interfered in "Previous Arab Region's Unity and common Market Formation"

Since the independence of many Arab countries from colonialism and the establishment of the Arab League there were several movements to bring unity and advancement to the region's various countries, by the establishment of "a united Arab common market", which was started way back in 1953. The movements were encouraged then by the many promoting, stimulus factors, which were expected to facilitate and speed up the formation of an Arab common market and region's union. They include use of Arabic as the official and daily-use language in each of the present 20 Arab World contiguous countries; the unity was further supported by the region population's dominance by the Islamic religion. For the last 14 centuries, population of the region shares also the same culture and history. The movement was especially encouraged and highly motivated by the ending and collapse of Arab region's European colonialism. A large number of the population has the nostalgia to revert back to the "United Arab Golden Age Era" with its huge, extended market. Another uniting stimulus is the "Arab League formation now includes all the 20 Arab countries as members; its charter is in favor and support of an Arab union [3]. Additionally, the majority of the Arab World population is looking forward for modernity, change and improvement of life, better employment, better education and economic conditions along with the freedom of movement and investment within the vast Arab World region. Still further support to the proposal can be found in the absence since early 1980s of military revolutions in the region. All these conditions were ripe and were also considered in support, strongly inducers of a regional pan Arab common market and union formation (for more detail on the subject see both Preface and Introduction Sections).

Even up to present time, the Arab governments still continued to advocate, during their Arab League Summits final declarations, to recommend and call for Arab unity and common market formation and development as was sought earlier. This repeated approach was also done during the very recent Doha Summit (March 2009) and other final Arab Summit declarations too; but unfortunately all so far, for many reasons no unity or total open common market status were accomplished, nor the expected gains and benefits that the region should have realized by this highly beneficial action. "The unity recommendations were short of neither a serious accompanying time line schedule nor a fixed procedure and budget for carrying and collectively implementing the recommended common market and unity tasks. The recommendations also ignored the very critical and extremely important role of the R&D-based techno-economic and simultaneously support education plan in the revival and development of the region technically and industrially from its present developing status (see Section on text's Summary)".

A summary of factors that were held responsible for delay of the proposed AU and common market formation is presented in this Section 6.3; while another summary of recent Arab unity and common market promoting stimuli is being presented and discussed in the following Sections (6.4) of this chapter. The latter summary represents the many now encountered local and geopolitical economical stimuli; some of them are entirely different from past issues. The summary of factors that were held responsible for delay of the proposed AU and common market formation is:

First, one of the greatest obstacles that in the past prevented Arab unity and the creation of Arab common market was the strong attachment and determination of each Arab government and Ruler's to retain country's independence and same form of government without change. The factor then was and continued until now very much the same nearly for all Arab government without exception. The situation as reported earlier tends to be a legitimately inheritance right case of father-to-son. In the past, many battles and wars were waged to preserve and maintain the now existing form of government. For example, we have seen how Iraq's occupation of Kuwait led to the first Gulf War and how foreign powers led by U.S.A resulted in free Kuwait, followed later on by the present Second Gulf War and the temporary occupation of Iraq.

*(**Now**, to emphasize again, the proposed "AU" modeled on "EU", enforces this more or less sacred rule - returning the independence and form of present government as it is now in Arab countries. Moreover, it allows legally and totally, full supports to this law without neither disturbing nor violating the concept).*

Second, the many earlier military revolutions (1948-1980) in the region to over through then the existing governments, with the false justification and premises that the objective of the junta, is to establish Arab unity and development of the region, which were never met. These revolutions placed then the ruling governments on the high alert status with emphasis on how to maintain the government and the country safe of military over-through. The ruler and the ruling government's top prime concern then was "how to maintain the government's rule" and were far less concerned with country's development and regional unity. Several Arab countries continue to suffer from the ill-effects of military revolution and military control, which remained dominant in many of them, up to present time.

The process of nationalization of private properties such as land and private industry, which presently is being reversed, exaggerated the situation by keeping both the local and foreign investment away from the region. In many instances, the net effect of the juntas' revolution was to send both the outside and local's - especially oil-rich Arab Gulf countries - excessive funds and investments elsewhere in search of   so-called safety outside the Arab region, mainly in advanced countries, Europe and U.S.

Definitely all these events not only prevented the region's unity but too stopped other foreign nations and enterprises from regional investment in particular in poor Arab countries; in addition it delayed considerably the development and investment within the region, although many people argue otherwise! The two actions - over through of then the existing government followed by nationalization of private properties - are now memory of the past. Now, there is some weak but insufficient tendency to   reverse the trend of investment by the oil-rich Arab and foreign nations in the poor Arab states. In spite of this change, unfortunately, still most of oil-rich Arab funds continued up to now their search for foreign investment in developed nations as evidenced by the many recent Arab Gulf funds investment and bailout of some U.S and EU's banks and enterprises – sometimes with major loss of Gulf Arab funds' investment.

*"Time for change of regional investment attitude; by replacing their earlier investment in advanced nations' market by making most of it in Arab countries, especially the poor ones, which now represent over 88% of the region's population. **Again**, the founding and development of the proposed Arab Union shall reverse the trend by attracting local and outside investment within the entire proposed Arab Union's region, with benefits and investment safety to all)".*

Third, since early days of Arab independence from European colonialism and the establishment of the Arab League in 1945 and up to present time, there have been many attempts to establish an Arab unity and common market. All these movements and unity attempts, however, as already indicated failed the Arab region to achieve unity and common market starts. In essence, the many calls for unity by then Arab ruling governments were simple repeated talk of promises; how they get away with it continues to puzzle many of the region's population (for more of the same see the Introduction to this section).

The above indecisive, no cooperative work of Arab governments and head of states' is in agreement with findings of earlier Monnet and UN's reports (see Section 6.2 reports [4, 5-11] on same subject). For example Monnet's findings on proposed Arab Union modeled on European Union as stated earlier, showed that Among European Union members a wide number of issues and variety of mutual union policies and institutionalization are discussed, including high degree of transfer of common issues and problems to the Union. While bargaining occurred, eventually leading to agreement and a widespread feeling of a common identity, mutual obligations and interest among the people of the European Union; the same indicators are only weakly present in the Arab region, especially Arab League Summit concluding recommendation. "Closer integration is hampered by the absence of a well-embedded institutional fabric, political commitment among the governments or leaders, and a transnational business culture seeking the establishment of economies of scale". In order to accomplish what the EU's countries have achieved the author concluded that the Arab integration needs to develop more strongly along the above EU lines. To promote such a development means that the Arab governments and population deal collectively with prevailing geo-political issues and circumstances. Furthermore, the author claimed that in the Arab World case "citizen participation and private sector initiative have remained constrained" [4], which needs to be revived and reformed in order to raise citizen participation in Arabs' domestic political and techno-economic affairs. It shall also provide a stop blaming ruling governments alone for delay of unity and common market development. Time is ripe for the awakening and engagement in the region's development to involve the whole population, government and governed segments in the techno-economic development of the whole region.

Fourth, to a great extent, the lack of Arab World nation union formation and common market's progress are due mainly, and perhaps principally, to inadequate Arab region's techno-economic planning. An appropriate, progressive planning calls for the creation of expanded Arabs' market and unity. Unlike the plans presently, routinely implemented by each and every one of the world developed advanced and emerging nations (see Chapters 3 & 4) the Arab World countries past annual and five year economic and industrial plans were nearly void and did not sufficiently include the very essential, necessary, innovative scientific, sustainable R&D-based techno-economic plans and programs nor the introduction of industries based on technology transfer processes. These plans, as repeatedly mentioned, were among the leading, critical factors responsible for the success story of all the advancements made by the advanced, developed and emerging countries.

The Arab World's very low, insignificant R&D efforts continued to be very much limited and extremely short in quality and quantity, ineffective toward improvement of Arab's science, technology, industry and economy and therefore were non-inductive neither to unity nor to open common market establishment. Proper R&D activity should have led the Arabs to a coordinated pan Arab efforts in development of their economy which in turn shall lead them also to: unity, progress, common market and techno-economic planning.

Very significant and extremely important is the total spending funds on R&D efforts, which are the core of advanced nations continued progress (see Chapters 3,4). As early mentioned, R&D funding by both the oil-rich and poor Arab nations continue to be very trivial; in year 2004 less than 0.2% GDP, for the whole Arab region. A meager ratio, dwarfed by the much higher ratio, spent by advanced nations. As shown in many of the earlier Tables 1-5 and Figure 1 in Chapter3, many other nations spend a much higher ratio, up to 3%- 5% of their GDP, on their R&D efforts than that spent by the Arab nations.

The number of Arab scientists and engineers per capita is a third of the world average! The number of computers per capita is a quarter of the global average – mainly in developing and emerging countries. Fewer than one in 20 Arab university students are pursuing scientific disciplines, while South Korea the figure is one in five. Arab countries have an estimated 371 research scientists and engineers per million citizens, compared to about three fold this figure for the global rate of 979 per million [7]. Furthermore, the level and result of their R&D efforts are far below that produced by their counterpart in developed or even emerging nations.

All these facts illustrate the degree of unnecessarily irrelevancy of R&D efforts and coordinated techno-economic plans in Arab World countries. If the Arab World looks forward toward changing their present status and techno-economic planning strategy, progressing technically, industrially and economically; they must   allocate, as shown later, much greater efforts and larger percentage of their GDP income toward R&D activities in various fields of science and technology; matching or exceeding (in order to catch up) what other advanced, developed and emerging nations' now spend on this extremely important R&D activity (for more detail see Chapter 6, Section 6.6).

According to reports commenting on the United Nations report [7-11], and our findings that the Arab region continues to fall behind not only when compared to the normally considered developed countries of the West, but also to the lately emerging developed nations in East Asia Pacific region, such as Taiwan, Singapore, China and India and South Korea, who have shown, as was illustrated in Chapter 4, a breathtaking expansion in science and technology coupled with rapid economic and industrial growth. By comparison, the present Arab' spending on research and development as given in Tables 1-5 Chapter 3 are an order of magnitude way below the global average. Some, as we do, argues that Arab World nations must take a big leap forward in developing science and technology to catch up with the rest of the world, or they risk falling behind in the global technology and economy processes [11].

(*This* *approach of techno-economic planning and industrialization, including creation of an open, free enterprise Arab common market, was not done properly nor implemented by Arab countries, failing them to achieve change and improvement of techno-economic and unity status.* *Can a* *leap forward similar to that of East Asia Pacific region occurs in the Arab world and why not; especially when they now posses all the means, technology stimulus (see following section) to perform this very important and extremely essential job and function? A catch-up process can be definitely accomplished by the founding and development of the proposed Arab Union, particularly since the world markets are open to purchase any requirements needed for the act.* **Shame**, *shame and more shame a region with many wealthy parts and glorious cultural past emphasizing scholarship and knowledge should never have been in this shameful unhealthy situation! Where are the bygone Arab generation that made knowledge, science and know how their ultimate goal in life and the development then of their society and status [24]*).

Fifth, the Arab world region unity and common open market efforts were greatly hampered by the method of Arab and foreign investment in and outside the region. During the latter part of the twentieth century and up to present time, only a limited capital investment from both local and foreign regions has been allocated to the various underdeveloped, oil non-rich Arab countries market, which is nowadays badly needed to assist the region in its techno-economic developmental plans.

Presently, because of lack of industry in the region, the Arab World exports a large portion of its wealth (capital and manpower) to developed countries. Manpower wealth is constituted mainly of university graduates. They are forced because of lack of jobs in none industrialized

Arab region to immigrate seeking opportunity and improved career, outside the region [12]. This double edge damaging process deprives the Arab region not only of investment to build industries and develop technology but also deprive it from the potentially skilled manpower to run them.

According to a new study by Cairo's Gulf Centre for Strategic Studies [12], "the emigration of scientists, disenchanted by factors ranging from a lack of investment in research to social and political instability in the region, is threatening the future technological and scientific development of the Arab world". The study found that the emigration of intellectuals from the Arab world accounts "for about one-third of the total 'brain drain' from developing countries to the West! Arab countries lose 15 per cent of scientists each year, with three quarters of these moving to the United Kingdom, United States and Canada". This estimated annual loss of Arab states is estimated at more than US $2 billion. The study also found that "45 per cent of Arab students who study abroad do not go back to their countries after graduating". As a result, it says that Western states are the greatest beneficiaries of "about 450,000 Arabs with higher scientific qualifications". Iraq, for example, is currently suffering a new brain drain as intellectuals flee out of the country to avoid unemployment and assassination attempts. Many other Arab countries are losing huge number of their scientists and engineers to the outside, with Palestine loosing nearly all of them. These problems shall be further exaggerated by the expected great rise in the region population, to doubling in number in couple of decades. The rise requires a matching jump in extra water, extra food, extra space to live and extra industry to work, build and develop.

The above cases - lack of investment in the region - contributed to the relatively high overall unemployment within the region, forcing many of its labor population to migrate [12]. For example, presently over 5 million people migrated to Europe from North African Arab countries alone. The Arab League meeting of June 2008, reported that the unemployment in many of the none oil-rich Arab countries reached about 25-30% and in some cases much higher, where for example it is over 60% in the Gaza region of Palestine.

The lack of local or foreign enterprise company's investment by Private Enterprise companies in the Arab region, especially in the poor part of Arab countries, nearly do not exist. Their presence is expected to contribute significantly to the region's industrialization, particularly its R&D efforts, wherein normally the free enterprise system contributes up to 60-70% of R&D budget (see Chapters 3 and 4). Business in various parts of Arab countries is controlled mostly either by government owned companies, such as the big oil companies, or family controlled companies, which so far as already proven, have low interest in developing technology. They activity engaged in trade promoting products made by foreign suppliers outside the region; additionally their trade is very much limited within the borders of their own country. The mostly family controlled business and private industry's negative attitude toward introduction and development of technology had contributed to the lack of industrialization within the region and is an important factor partially responsible for lack of technology and knowledge development in the Arab World; they - some of the families get richer while majority of the people get poorer.

(The regions "capacity to absorb investment" shall rise significantly by the founding and development of the proposed Arab Union. The question why this important work was not previously done in spite of the wealth – capital and manpower - which were invested outside the region instead of being invested within it? Additionally, *the founding and development of the proposed Arab Union shall attract local and outside investment including free enterprise companies within the proposed Arab Union region).*

Sixth, apart from economic and political causes that hinder education and industrialization in Arab countries, some claim that the near hostility attitude of some elements in Islam and Arab societies to modernity plus their misinterpretation of religion stand on the way of region's advancement and scientific development . On the subject of religion, they suggest that oppressive regimes and conservative religious scholars have colluded to produce "certain interpretations of Islam" that represent "serious impediments to human development, particularly when it comes to freedom of thought, accountability of the ruling authorities, and women's participation in public life. Some advocate calls for "delivering pure religion from political exploitation and respecting independent scholarship." They further also recommend "reclaiming the intellectual strengths of Arab cultural heritage; promoting cultural diversity in the region; and opening up to other cultures abroad [5]". Some advocate calls for "delivering pure religion from political exploitation and respecting independent scholarship."

True, somehow these above groups unjustified stand is partially responsible for the absence of industry and advanced new essential research in variety of fields, but the major cause is the lack of Arab political and economic, industrial and R&D-based techno-economic work that led to the low progress in the region. Truly, the Arab countries did not carry the same activities. Excuses given to justify their failure are not acceptable; it is time to correctly claim that they failed. Blaming tyrants and extremists for religious intolerance is insufficient to stop the above claimed intervention. It is well known that the governments stops all undesired activities against them, they equally can easily stop all actions designed by religious fanatical, zealous extremist or any other groups interfering with nation's progress and development. The Arab countries must disregard the very wrong irreligious views and completely stop their advocates from actually hurt the nation's economy. Anyway, the claims themselves are completely none Islamic, non-religious in nature and manner. Definitely, those who believe and advocate the above concept have it wrong (for more detail on the subject see Chapter 5, Section 5.3.1)!

The same above claims although were practiced during the Europeans' dark ages, we see them now practiced side-by-side with the monotheistic Christianity along with the highly impressive techno-economic EU progress and advancement. The same was also true and practiced during the Arab Golden Age Era, 750-1300; wherein progress and development of science, knowledge and know-how existed then side-by-side with monotheistic Islamic religion. Let us remember that Islamic teaching, emphasized **"Read, Write and perform R&D"** in first

Qur'an Ayah to Muslims prior to any others including the five important compulsory pillars of Islam. Numerous Qur'an Ayahs and prophet's Hadeaths - saying and teachings - are in support of learning and development of science and knowledge (see Chapter 5, Sections 5.3 and 5.3.1). All these Islamic teachings were among the biggest stimuli that allowed for developing of knowledge, science and know how during the Arab Golden Age Era and beyond as well (for more detail on the subject see Chapter 5, Section 5.3)!

The region is way behind advanced nations and the world in many relevant fields such as: information technology, molecular biology, chemistry and physics, biotechnology, nano-technology, stem cell technologies, genomics, pharmaceuticals, energy, software development, electronics, etc. Application of such research could have directed the Arabs to new rich markets and industries in addition to many healthy benefits to humans.

I may also emphasize that during my long 30 years R&D work in the Arab region, I never encountered any religious objection to my R&D work; in fact it was highly admired and many endorsed and supported it. *So, it can be concluded that religion cannot be claimed any longer as a technology hindering factor; rather correct interpretation of Islamic religion place it in strong support and stimulus of an R&D-based techno-economical activity including the founding and development of the proposed Arab Union - see Section 5.3.1.*

Seventh, after Arab independence the UN report and comments on it notes that: "most Arab countries came under national political regimes that represented little advance on the autocratic style of ancient and more recent history" [5, 7-11]. As a result, social and individual freedoms have been curtailed and restricted. There is a "political and social context in many occasions opposed to the development of science". It warns that "Arab societies are being crippled by a lack of political freedom, the repression of women and isolation from the world of ideas that stifles creativity. In one part of the same U.N. report [5] the team leader, Fergany, stated that "A person who is not free is poor. A woman who is not empowered is poor. And a person who has no access to knowledge is poor."By all these criteria, "the Arab region—even some of its wealthiest corners—could only be described as impoverished"!

Moreover, "with many economies dependent on oil production and exportation, little value is given to culture, education" [5], and development of knowledge as well as technology. The reports note that while oil income has transformed the landscapes of some Arab countries, the region remains "richer than it is developed". The "per capita income growth" and currency buying of majority of Arab population of nearly about 88% "has shrunk in the last 20 years, prior to 2007, to a level just above that of sub-Saharan Africa".

True these above issues including the "autocratic style of governments" may interfere with the very low progress in Arab region, but *again, as reported under above item sixth, it was the lack and negligence of an R&D-based techno-economic development plans that kept the region away from developing science and technology. The case is made very clear again by China's action and industrialization; now the second richest world nation in GDP and R&D spending. China is not only none democratic, but it is also militarily ruled with only one communist party system. Yet their awareness of the techno-economic plan led them to apply it reaching their present spectacular progress. The Arab government's main requirement for the region's progress and success is   to pursue other developed nations techno-economic plans. The region shall be immensely improved and changed to advanced case only by the establishment of the proposed AU. Moreover, that leaders and heads of government will be greatly treated and respected as great reformers, loved by the population for the economic advancement they are able to accomplish).*

Eighth, the UNDP report [5] that lack of "an intelligent and generous exchange with non-Arab cultures and civilizations" has a great effect on both Arab and non-Arab countries. The same report recommends reclaiming the intellectual strengths of Arab cultural heritage; promoting cultural diversity in the region; and opening it up to other cultures abroad. The present lack in information exchange rose first from the absence of cooperation and union among the various Arab World countries, followed second by the Arab region's inferior accomplishment in science, technology and industrialization. Very important also, it was generated from region's failure to develop an up-to-date advanced R&D-based techno-economic plan as proposed here. The initiative requires Arab researcher's involvement and development in worthwhile projects and programs of communal and scientific interest to both the Arab and foreign partners. The action would have lead to development of an authentic, enlightened Arab knowledge model, which can be worthwhile to exchange with others working in same fields within advanced societies.

Again, while working in the region I never was away from total engagement in information exchange with my counter part researchers working worldwide in the same field. By contrast, because of the relevance of my R&D and its general contribution to development of knowledge in my R&D field, I had enormous cooperative R&D projects and programs: over 5 years with top researchers from GKSS of Germany representing their R&D ministry; many other years of cooperation and joint work with U.S. Bureau of Reclamation; several other years of R&D cooperation with Japan's International Cooperation Agency (JICA) and many other companies involved in R&D activities plus exchange of information with thousands working in R&D and tech development, mainly in seawater desalination. These various R&D activities were jointly initiated: a great number of which were through my special personnel R&D efforts (see about the Author), others through inter-government relations and agreements with free enterprise companies. But in all cases for *proper R&D information's exchange within Arab or with outside foreign regions, Arab researchers must initiate the activity in full support and engagement of both government and private sector, which should be relevant and worthwhile to them and foreign cooperation.*

Many of the writers on the subject call for the revival of an optimal techno-economic regional conditions and Arab re-contribution to science, knowledge and technology (see Chapter 5, Section 5.3). Why cannot the Arab World countries utilize all these measures to promote R&D and development of technology, especially when they now possess all the means, stimuli and the power – capital and potentially skilled manpower - to perform this very important and extremely essential, detrimental, developmental job and function? Could the Arab governments and population with help of Arab League and the proper techno-economic assistance aid the region to overcome the above obstacles that in the past hindered unity and common market formation? To perform this responsibility by the encouragement and development of knowledge, technology and science the United Nations Development Program (UNDP) on the Arab Human Development 2002 Report recommended and introduces "the Arab knowledge society", five pillars, having analogy to the Islamic religion obligatory five pillars, making knowledge as a religious duty as it was nearly the same during the Arab/ Muslim Golden Age Era. They are [5, 14-17]:

- "Guaranteeing the key freedoms of opinion, speech and assembly through good governance bounded by the law. The report affirms that a climate of freedom is an essential prerequisite of the knowledge society".

(Arab governments and population can do the same without democracy even in presence of existing rules (see above earlier discussion on the subject). What is important and extremely relevance in this case is to reform the techno-economic plan, giving it the support and capability to perfume the task of advancing the region from developing to developed status as for example China did).

- "The full dissemination of high quality education. The report calls for basic education to be universal and extended to 10 years. It recommends that special attention be paid to early childhood learning and to creating a system for lifelong learning".

(Education program, however, must be compatible with AU plan in order to produce the required skilled manpower to run and operate it).

- "Promoting homegrown science and research and development, and joining the Information Revolution. The report calls for research to be encouraged through funding and institutions. Arab governments should also establish networks linking public, private and international sectors", (See Section 6.6).

- "Shifting rapidly toward knowledge-based and value-added production. This means developing knowledge and technological capabilities and diversifying economic structures and markets".

- "Developing an authentic, broad-minded and enlightened Arab knowledge model. The report calls for "delivering pure religion from political exploitation and respecting independent scholarship." It also recommends reclaiming the intellectual strengths of Arab cultural heritage; promoting cultural diversity in the region; and opening up to other cultures abroad".

(As already indicated Islam as well as other monotheistic religions is science and techno-economic promoter and should be guarded and protected from misinterpretations of overzealous wrong interpreters and political exploitation).

One additional 6th pillar must be added by the authors, who share their views on the subject:

- Making acquisition of knowledge through the R&D process an **<u>obligatory</u>** duty, part of Islam religious work (see Chapter 5, Section 5.3.1).

(Why not considering the improvement of living conditions by improving region's technological and economic status the way they now (the Muslims) overemphasize and practice prayer? It is not only how many times you kneel through prayers but equally true how much your good R&D and innovative work can help other humans – Muslim or none Muslim - to survive, enjoying the progress and beauty of happy life).

6.4 Summary of Local, Geopolitical and Economical Stimuli Promoting Formation and Development of the Proposed Arab Union

How can they - the Arab countries - revive their present economy and technology and depart away from the old traditional economic planning that kept the region classified a developing region in spite of the great wealth in excess high capital in some parts especially the oil-rich Arab countries, and abundant manpower, land and resources in most of the region? There are several promoting stimuli - as given in this section - that shall stimulate the region finally to be ready to depart away from its old economic and developmental planning approach; allow it to exchange present status with modern planning as now recommended in the proposal by the establishment of a total Arab regional common market, operated and controlled through Arab Union modeled after the highly successful European Union. We arrived at this conclusion, which is supported by the following recent local and foreign development trends and moves, all calling and influencing   the future region's economical cooperative and developmental planning decisions:

First, the many heads of Arab Mediterranean countries, which represent a majority of Arab population (about 221 million out of total of over 329 million), attended the Paris Summit, made no surprise to many observers that they, the Arabs, were looking forward for such union to succeed, achieving the "UM" goals. Their initial fast approval of "UM" showed the great relevancy of the union to the Arab region and more so enforced the assumption that   at last the Arabs who attended the Paris Summit are tentatively in support of Union formation even with their neighbors. Presumably, the Mediterranean Arabs, considered such union of major advantage and of great benefit to the revival and improvement of the saddened, developing case of the Arab' nations economy and population. Additionally, it too established a   stronger needed communication and cooperation with an obviously friendly, highly advanced neighbor, with both the European and the Arab Mediterranean states sides gaining great benefit from the union.

Second, There exists now urgent need for R&D work in the Arab region to perform multitude of activities in variety of fields to develop the necessary technology and tools to solve the many problems that kept the region behind in this digital age. A summary list is given in Chapter 6, Section 6.6 on how to increase and greatly enhance R&D efforts, intensity and funding at a fast pace in the region that badly need it. The required activity has been considerably enhanced within the region, wherein some remarkably recent, positive movements are being witnessed in the Arab world. Saudi Arabian Kingdom is to increase research and development spending to 2.5% of GDP from its relatively low ratio of 0.2-0.5% of GDP, for a total of over SR 32 billion ($8.6 billion) as part of its 20-year National Science and Technology Plan [20]. The recent $10 billion endowment introduced by "Sheikh Mohammed bin Rashid Al-Maktoum Foundation" constitutes another means of promoting R&D efforts in the Arab World. The foundation has set goals to promote human development in the region with emphasis on R&D, science and technology development [21]. The R&D activity is required to allow for both a critical catch –up with other advanced nations and also to give the region the ability to solve many of its severe financial, social and techno-economic problems. These important activities are required also to raise countries' industrialization and techno-economic development as well as being central, essential and critically required tools for the proposed AU success.

Third, Since the independence of many Arab countries from colonialism (1945-1980) and the establishment of the Arab League there were several movements to bring unity and advancement to the region's various countries, by the establishment of "a united Arab common market". These unity and common market movements are now encouraged by the recent Doha (March 2009) Arab Summits; the heads of Arab States called for Arab unity, recommended the long waited for, "a total Arab countries common, open free enterprise trade market". Other final Arab Summit declarations too called for many other forward Arab unity measures to be taken, including better economic and political coordination among the region's countries [26]. The above proposed work is in conformity with the initiative being proposed here: formation and development of AU modeled after EU. Both initiatives of revival of Arab common market as proposed in Doha Summit and AU are certain to yield great progress in presence of such great regional wealth of capital and manpower, readiness of EU and other advanced nations to aid (upon Arab countries request) in establishment and development of AU. Definitely, this work is necessary, extremely essential in order to avoid future population's complication for both the present and the greatly expanding future generations.

Fourth, as was convened by other advanced world powers: G8, G7, EU and the top 20 richest nations to deal with subject of the present financial and economic crisis, the heads of the 20 Arab World countries, had their joint Summit Arab Economic Conference in Kuwait (January 2009). Their gathering was the first to be held on such a topic, which again suggests the region's awareness and sort of collective cooperation in confronting such difficult and very serious regional and world economic crisis problem. Recently there was a great deal of coordination in solving differences in joint problems between various Arab countries, especially after major war incidents in the region such as: the Israel invasion of Gaza, where the GCC Gulf countries pledged about $2 billion aid to Gaza reconstruction; the Sudanese conflict gave rise to Qatar peace proposal among conflicting Sudanese factions, the Syrian-Lebanese disputes and most recently the Syrian-Iraqi coordination Summit (August 17, 2009). Both the Syrian president and Iraqi prime minister discussed bilateral cooperation between Syria and Iraq and the importance of bolstering relation and cooperation in all fields; particularly cooperation in politics, economy and security including everything that secures the interests of the two countries, their peoples and preserve the two countries and Arabian region's stability in general.

Fifth, Definitely there is now great awareness by the region's government and population for unity such as advanced in the present AU's proposal. Development of such enterprise is beneficial to all regions' citizens: government or private sector. Regions' progressive, advance economy becomes the controlling and guiding principle; bringing wealth, progress and comfort to all government and governed population (see previous Item 4). It shall overcome all differences in the now economic rich and poor states, ideological groups Sunnis versus Shiites or fundamentalist versus moderate forms of religion, Arab majority versus non-Arab minority and political royal or republican as well. With the exception of the will and determination, proper coordination, negotiation and compromise to perform this very important task,   we believe that the Arab region possesses nearly all the necessary tools to perform this very important R&D-based techno-economic task.

We strongly believe along with great region's majority that there is a critical need to introduce the proper progressive change reviving the economy and industrialization of the region. The movement requires the joint cooperation and participation of both the government and the private non-government sector not only to recognize and learn how over the past 5 decades many poor nations acquired advanced economical status but also work hard to install the same reforms within the region to transfer its economy from developing to advanced status. They must also know that the Arab region is now in a far superior position than many of these nations were when they decided to take the venture, the challenge and the transformation step. With the appropriate region's coordination and sincere cooperation, the achievement is within the reach and the successful guarantee of Arab countries, especially to reemphasize in presence of the numerous local and foreign political and economical stimuli; so why not to do it? "**They planted for us and we ate; and we shall plant for future ones also to eat**"!

Sixth, There exists also additional reasons for the Arab region to stand up to the challenge, satisfying the great beneficial strategy hidden in the formation and development of the proposed Arab Union and common market. Consider **first** the **European Union** formation. It was completed and now constituted a success story in spite of member countries speaks a variety of languages, differ somewhat in culture, they have great variety of religious sects. The EU was also established as already mentioned following many disastrous wars that created enmity between citizens who now post EU founding are friendly, highly cooperative neighbors and EU citizens; the region now acquired large degree of assimilation and integration. In addition to that the European Union was accomplished between then the rich developed Western European and the far less developed, relatively less rich South, Central and Eastern European countries.

For a **second** example let us, consider the first **U.S. 14 States Federation** between then the industry rich Northern and the mostly relatively far less rich, agricultural Southern States. The United States of America completed the union to now 50 States by having as members many desert and far less developed states then as well. Eventually with passage of time, and considerable efforts, guidance, help and aid by the more developed to the less developed part of the union, equilibrium in wealth and gradually developed nations' status were established in both cases- EU and U.S.A- along with the disappearance of the differences that originally divided them. Can any one imagine U.S or EU state of economy without the union? U.S. Civil War was necessarily waged to keep and maintain the federation. The European Union does not need to do that, many European and non- European countries are literarily fighting to join EU membership and under the rules and command of EU. Since EU founding no European nation has left the union.

It can be equally argued **thirdly** that the numerous religions, wealth, political, military and developmental issues differences [4 and 5] did not stop both the European and U.S.A from forming EU or U.S Federation. It can be **fourthly** argued too that the advancements now witnessed in China and other countries- population over 1.3 billion - were achieved in spite of military rule in the country. Same argument, token and logic can be extended also to the Arab region's population case to enhance unity and common market establishment since they now possess many of the unity promoting stimuli. *(But, would the Arab region duplicate this same very smart act - forming AU and common market - and why not?)*

There is now no stressing obligation to delay neither the unity nor the common Arab market starts any longer; it must be done now and immediately following the EU model style. They - the region considering their economic and industrial situation - deserve such Arab Union, blessed by neighbors and can't be stopped by foes. As it was very speedily and smoothly done in the establishment of UM between Arabs and EU countries, it can be equally similarly done by the Arabs - the establishment and implementation of such highly beneficial AU undertaking initiative between brothers' Arab countries and population. It is only the collective Arab determination that decides on the happening of this AU great initiative. Definitely, the unity and common market move shall out-weigh the very, very small benefits, division and uncooperative status presently existing among most of Arab countries. By contrast, "lack of such unity and common market shall maintain and leave the majority of Arab population - now 88% - in excessive poverty and unemployment, misery and despair, disorder and terror; suffering from the present high deficiency in techno-economic, scientific, educational and social progress". Furthermore, **all the claimed and in many cases assumed present hurdles now standing in the way of Arab Union (see previous Section 6.3) shall completely disappear upon the Arab Union and common market foundation.** Very important, the Arab Union and common market formation is not only just in complete conformity and full support of the entire region's development and economic progress but it is also equally in full conformity and maintenance of existing government's political system, independence and form of government as well; look how well and progressive are EU, and USA and other nations that followed the correct, modern techno-economic plan.

All the above arguments and discussions together with many other union promoting present regional and international stimuli are more than sufficient to convince all Arab countries - governments and governed population - to initiate a fresh and serious approach toward the formation, implementation and completion of an Arab Union with EU aid and assistance. The AU is further supported by the following summary of the many presently existing, additional encouraging; local and foreign promotional stimuli for the formation of the proposed AU common market community:

First and foremost, the way they are divided now, they - various Arab region countries and population - are fully subjugated to dominant foreign powers' decisions. Without a total union, they shall remain extremely sensitive, very much exposed and influenced by those mighty powers' decision and ambitions in controlling the region, especially its natural resources' wealth. Since independence, they were first dominated in many parts of Arab land by either the French or British followed later by U.S.S.R and U.S.A domination and most recently they are now dominated mostly by U.S.A shared by others. The region's unity - formation of AU specifically modeled on EU - provides the region with one of the biggest incentive to offset this undesired situation and intervention of foreign powers in region's affairs, replacing it as was done now among advanced nations with full amicable negotiation, coordination and understanding. Rather than conflict, misunderstanding and disorder, progressive rich trade - as now exist among advanced and emerging nations/regions - then becomes the guiding rule and issue between them united and dominant powers. It shall give the vast, populated region the strength, the stance and the international power and prestige to make their free decision and say. The unity shall also protect the region and each member country from local or outside interference or invasion as now was done in Iraq's occupation. The move also facilitates, encourages trade, exchange of knowledge and know how within the region and the rest of the world. All problems within or outside the region can be solved amicably, as was done now at EU, without the region resorting to force or parts of it exposed to foreign interference or even occupation.

A **Seventh** great incentive and stimulus for the formation of AU is the great wealth acquired by the oil rich Arab countries, especially now, with a spectacular rise in price of oil, sometimes in excess of $140/barrel, now continued high in excess of $65-70/barrel. "**Should this wealth** as already suggested earlier (see Chapter 5, Section 4; also Chapter 2, Section 1) be spent - exported - outside the region as was done in the past, leaving the region non-industrialized, underdeveloped?" **Or** "should the Arab community unite by the formation of AU as proposed here, assisting each others, in utilizing this wealth wisely to stimulate investment of most of the oil revenues to revive all the Arab region; to fund investment in building and developing a healthy highly progressive R&D-based techno-economic industrial plan, rich community with benefits to all rich and poor Arabs as well as its neighbors and the world?" Moreover, the wealth of the region allows it the acquisition of all needed equipments, factories, local and foreign experts' manpower from the world free open markets. At the same time, each of the region's countries maintains, as repeatedly emphasized, a safe, secure population, retaining - without having to wage a war - same state independence and same government form in addition of safe investment as being done now in EU region.

Many oil-rich Arab funds are now in search for an investment foreign home, with the danger of great loss as now happened to many Arab Gulf countries investment funds - their present investment loss is estimated in excess of $400 billion(see internet) - which came as a result of present world financial and economic crisis! Why not consider investing it to develop the Arab region, with great benefits to all Arabs, rich and poor, rulers and governed private citizens? At the same time the investors retain investment rights, revenues and share profits, secure by the proposed AU; saving   the region the evil of unemployment, the evil of poverty, the evil of shortage in life-essential matter as well avoiding sickness and starvation, disease, etc. Morally, ethically and economically and as repeatedly advised by friendly and opposing heads of other states (see Chapter 5, Section 4),   they must invest within the region, assisting less privileged Arab brothers' countries overcome poverty - now constituting over 88% of the region population and eventual benefit to all.

Equally true is that the excessive, massive number of potentially skilled manpower - graduates from home and abroad' universities – should be utilized in developing the techno-economic status of the region. Now, a good portion of this wealth is not properly utilized, while another large fraction of it is exported, as already indicated, together with large part of region's capital outside the region; making the region the largest world exporter of both. Among many nations of the globe, this qualified manpower represents their major   wealth that brought advancement and progress to the nation. Japan and Israel cases – both with minimum of natural resources - are excellent examples which fully utilizes this manpower as its main wealth; they seriously maintain it and do not export it.

Major causes leading to this case of manpower exporting is that the present Arab world industrial and economic situation did not allow for their absorption and utilization in a mainly nonindustrial, agricultural economy. The university graduate themselves are searching and looking for work to develop a career; nationally and naturally they are anxious to contribute to the region's development. By itself, stopping this wasteful manpower and capital's export is a great stimulus to drive the region to form the Arab Union and common market, which shall not only allow for capital investment within the region but also utilize the manpower in region's development as well as it, shall also lead to additional foreign investment in the region. In the long run, the initiative is beneficial to the region, its neighbors and the world.

Equally **Eighth** supporting stimulus for the formation of an AU and the development of an Arab World Common Market is that the population shares the same culture. For about 14 centuries, the region was part of the great Arab empires (634-1258) and thereafter part of the various other Arab/Muslim kingdoms or government's civilization and culture (1258-1800). The imperial, colonial rule of most of the region during the 19th and early part of the 20th century, although resulted in the partition of most of the region to its present country borders and states, they did not interfere in nor were able to change the region's population use of their language or religion, which they continue to use up to now.

Use of Arabic as the official language in each of the 20 Arab World countries continue to be a big stimulus for bringing solid Arabic communication and therefore unity, understanding and the collective development of the region. More people now see the "Al-Jazirah Arabic TV station" than their own local, national TV stations. The   unity is further supported by the dominance of Islamic religion of the region's population; only a very small percentage of the population follows the other monotheistic Christian faith, most of them, however, are of Arabic origin, great supporters of an AU formation. (Arabic was and continues to be the official language of the region promoting unity and love of all residents).

A **Ninth** great incentive stimulus is that the proposed AU charter as already stated, leaves each member of the 20 countries intact, retaining each country independence and form of government as it is now, with peace, security, investment and free movement to all. These rights, investment and benefits are collectivity guaranteed by the "AU" charter laws and all member countries. Alone, as already mentioned, this issue constitutes a very important, critical stimulus unity condition of great attraction, satisfaction and concern to all and every Arab governments, without any exception.

Additionally, by far the most important advantage of this stimulus will be the prevention of future major local conflicts within the region or out side it with dominant powers in search of wealth and resources. As done now in EU, where no major or war conflict has risen during the last 5 decades, the AU purposely selected model solve all disputes among member countries, local or foreign, amicably peacefully according to laws of the union, without having any member to resort to violence or war and as is practiced now in some cases. By itself, this last benefit deserves that the outside mighty powers too help the Arabs in quickly establishing and developing AU - simply in order to avoid the region's local or foreign highly anticipated, wasteful, evil and disastrous conflicts, which in many cases interfered with oil and trade flow and interruption of peaceful life and country's order.

A **Tenth** incentive stimulus for the formation of AU is the benefits gained from the union of creating a very large as mentioned, extensive free enterprise market open to all members. The proposed AU market covers vast land, 12.9 million square km, bordering 2 huge oceans and 3 great seas one of which- the Mediterranean - is enormously large. The total coastal land of sea shores are about 23,000 km, which is of great significant to a region that suffers greatly from water shortage. The land itself is contiguous and occupies a very important world central location between 3 continents; it is part of 2 of them. Total population of the 20 countries' region is presently in excess of 329 million and is expanding at an alarming rate; it is expected to reach double this number within the coming two decades.

Although rise in population's number should lead to a greater market expansion, the issue, however, is further complicated with passage of time, if the region fails to secure and establish

AU. The region's present acute shortages in two life-essentials (fresh water, and food production) plus other serious shortages in industrial and technological developments shall multiply. In order to avoid exposure of future generation to this shortage' problems, the situation require the region to match the population expansion with large increase in having additional requirements. The anticipated shortage case forces the region to stimulate and inspire a solution for it. The solution can be found and fully satisfied   by the proposed "AU" formation, developing the necessary R&D technology and right planned economy to counteract the problems of a crowded future Arab generation.

An **Eleventh** stimulus for AU formation is the anticipated EU willingness when requested to provide the necessary advice and technical aid required in catalyzing   the AU process. This willingness was recently demonstrated in forming the "Union of Mediterranean nation Initiative". The aid-step is very essential and necessary because so far the region failed to achieve the act alone. Very important in the past, the EU countries were a major cause of Arab World countries splitting into 20 different, non-cooperative countries. In order to remedy the problem, it becomes essential and more so obligatory that EU correct the Arab countries' splitting case by providing the proper, necessary aid that puts the region back together united again! The move and the aid shall stop the Arabs blaming the European for the present Arab splitting and in consequence their present sad economical status.

The EU shall be a major beneficiary too of this consulting aid to Arab nations. The aid shall secure flow of oil and gas from the region to EU, increase EU trade with the proposed "AU" Arab nation; also it shall minimize or even completely stop flow of Arab immigrant to Europe. Overall, the aid initiative shall be of further benefits to other world powers, to the whole world and shall contribute to stop local and foreign conflicts within the region.

Stopping of conflicts is of great importance to the region and world order as well. Presently, the region is witnessing a great degree of unrest, conflicts in some cases leading to disastrous wars or disastrous terror, which no one wants and calls for. Change, however, by improving the overall conditions of the people's employment and economy is what the region now requires. As accomplished by other nations in solving similar problems that confronted them in the past by the formation of unionized common open market, giving them peace and security along with employment; the same great stimulus approach can be utilized to deliver the same goods, benefits and advantages to the Arab region. The formation and implementation of a successful Arab Union is in full conformity with the regions' government and population demand for peace and security and change to a better life and pleasant future for all.

Presently **Twelfth**, part of the population is looking for change, modernity, improvement of life and economic conditions along with the freedom of movement and investment across the huge Arab land. Additionally, a great segment of the Arab population became aware of progress made by other developed nations, especially after the recent introduction of the modern information technology. Many of the region intellectuals - who are aware of their ancestors contribution to world of knowledge and science, the great unity and huge open market of the medieval Arabs - continued to work on stimulating Arab unity to see it effectively working again. Their main concern is how to awaken the Arab region - government and people - to carry on this humane unity mission, particularly its contribution to knowledge and aid to poor world nations (see reference 5).

The above list of 7 items represents the major promotional stimuli for the AU and common market initiative's establishment and development. Additional AU's promotional stimuli factors contributing to the same initiative are:

- One great unity promotional factor is that the region has its Arab League, established 1945, first with 7 States, and now includes all the 20 Arab countries as members plus 3 other countries out side the Arab region. Its main goals and charter calls among many regional collaboration and cooperation for: "the League shall co-ordinate economic affairs, including commercial relations; communications; cultural affairs; nationality, passports, and visas; social affairs; and health affairs"; it further forbids member states from resorting to use of force against each other. Indeed, the Arab League, although the charter may require certain amendments, still it calls for Arab Economic Union. The charter provides a strong stimulus and power and definitely no objection for the establishment of AU. The Arab League could play an active, major role in this regard by assisting in the formation of the "AU and regional economic and trade unity", as already recommended. We see no reason to stop "AL" from expanding their economic and unity activities, especially when both the proposed AU formation and league charter allow each country to retain and preserve its independence and form of government. *(The puzzling question is why didn't the Arab League management carry such economic unity role in the past?)*

- As discussed earlier in Chapter 5, Section 5.3.1, because of their high relevancy to human life, the use of the 4 religious Islamic principles **(Read, Write and perform R&D)** forms inductive impetus and stimulus act to push the region - people dominated by Islamic religion - to move forward to adopt R&D technology development which can be achieved by the establishment of the proposed AU. This strong religious stimulus for the acquisition of knowledge by the development of AU is further supported by the numerous Qur'an Ayahs and the Prophet's saying and teachings (Hadeath). These teachings and instructions were and continue to be among the major reasons - part of obligatory Islamic religion - for the realization of true Islam and the Arab Golden Age Era. The acts are in conformity that religion - in this case Islam - push the region to move forward, developing R&D technology and establish the region's AU. Further more, it is quite interesting to see that the United Nations Development Program (UNDP) on the Arab Human Development 2002 Report [5] recommended "the five pillars of an Arab knowledge society", in analogy to the Islamic five pillars (see Chapter 5, Section 5.3).

- Recent years have seen -what considered being- a significant economic growth in the Arab World; due to rise in price of oil and the efforts by some states to some how diversifying their economic base. Many achievements as already reported were gained by the region: building of cities many of which are new, new fancy commercial centers, health care, educational centers wherein the region now has over 100 universities; improved agriculture and many others among region's achievements. Industrial production has risen, especially in significant production of petroleum and petrochemical products and steel production [32]. (*Why not extend these activities to a total Arab open common market and Arab union establishment?*)

One encouraging recent inductive impetus movement by some Arab nations demonstrates that finally some of the Arabs are awakening to realize that increasing investments and greater involvement in R&D is very essential for the regional technology development, as presently being done by the Saudi Arabian government and U.A.E (see detail discussion of these two initiatives presented in earlier part of this section). The remaining Arab countries could follow the same approach, although of greater beneficial synergetic effect if the act is done collectively by all countries under   a unified Pan Arab Union R&D common community program, which can be achieved by the establishment of AU. The move is still positive and in the right direction. In spite of these above forward moves, "**what the region needs now: is to perform a fast-tracked unionized act by the formation of the proposed AU to address the stressing R&D and progressive economical efforts in the region; also to allow it to catch-up with advanced nations as well**".

- Many of the issues that supposedly interfered with earlier Arab unity formation and technology development (as noted in Section 6.3), their solutions and means to overcome them are now within the reach of nearly most Arab regions' government rulers. The present governments in many Arab countries grant or allow the ruler the means to pass and   decree the laws and regulations that permit funding, implementation and completion of the necessary rules and regulation as a ruler's macramah act. (In Arabic macramah means noble, high quality deed or grant and favorite act given to the people - in this case by the leader). R&D-based techno-economic plans and other regulation can be similarly introduced in form of macramah, if the leader wishes, can also grant them also top priority measures. This privilege constitutes still another stimulus to pass AU formation, which is presently enhanced by the great availability of wealth within parts of the region; so why not to use this ruler's gifted macramah to improve R&D and economic situation in the countries and region?

- The expected change induced by the region formation of AU, shall cause a great rise in region's wealth and progress to all including the minorities that live in the Arab word. This fact - introduction of AU - pushes the minority toward a healthy integration within the various parts of the AU and its common market, eventually leading them to complete assimilation and full integration within the Arab world, with great benefits to all. The great assimilation of variety of races, faiths and non-religious believers in U.S.A and other parts of the world are examples.

- The great cultural heritage that the region has, including the cradle of western civilization countries as well as the land where the three monotheistic religions originated, now with more than 54% of worldwide followers, the influence of both makes the Arab region one of the greatest pilgrimage/tourist attraction worldwide. The countries division and disputes interfere in the regional tourist market development and shared tourism benefits. On the other hand Regional industrialization and regional technical and economical development as well as openness and unity of the region resulting from AU establishment, make the place a far better and safer one to visit and live in than the present prevailing conditions; all of these conditions constitute great stimuli, forcing AU establishment. The "Arab Union" formation is expected to greatly improve regional overall status, generate an influx of tourists to the region with major economical gain.

Putting all these above positive promoting stimuli parameters and factors together with region's technical and economical needs along with earlier discussion on the same subject force us to recommend that "in order for the Arabs to have their independent thought and decision; establish progress, development acquiring improved developed nations status; establish peace and security throughout the region; solve their many shortages in life-essential requirements; avoid terror acts and problems; there is no excuse as well as no way out for them not to adopt and fully implement the above proposed "Arab Union" modeled on EU; union of countries, retaining their independence and form of government as it is now". All their assumed excuses for present statuesque shall be of insignificant value compared to the huge benefits and improvement gained by the region's AU establishment.

How else can they develop the region without AU founding by the use of both the present huge: capital wealth flowing now to parts of the region and the very great annual number of university graduates and other labor it produces annually and the tremendous resources that need to be developed? How else can they without the establishment of AU also meet the challenge of avoiding future great shortages in life-essential within the region, fight the potentially increased conflicts, the expected large increase in population, severe unemployment and other unexpected problems and terror? The population, both government and private are also desiring and looking forward for change, stability, security and peace, improvement that is expected to reverse the Arabs present situation, preventing all anticipated regional conflicts and problems. As being demonstrated by a huge number of cases, then poor and now advanced nations; no other act surpass and can perform the job better than the formation and implementation of the proposed united "AU" specifically modeled on "EU".

The above facts led us also to the conclusion that only through use and rigid implementation of advanced R&D-based techno-economic plans, simultaneously coupled with the appropriate educational and economic systems that all advanced and emerging nations without exception were able to advance and progress. Neither democracy nor supportive religious attitude, as frequently believed by many, although very helpful and desired and in many cases are now source of troubles; nevertheless their presence was not always essential, necessity for techno-economic progress as already demonstrated by the great China achievement and many others. Government's tolerance and love are strongly enhanced in presence of good advance economy; meanwhile absence of such factor generates the case of intolerance and disorder to both the government and population, again regardless of governments' form.

Finally, we also want the present Arabs and Governments again and again to remember with presumably great benefits to them and their societies of: First, how their great ancestors of the "Arab Golden Age Era" managed to be masters of their destiny, ruling and dominating a huge free open market; through use and development of knowledge, science and know how. We would like them also to remember Second: how many other countries - the Asia-Pacific ridge countries, Japan and China as well as EU plus many others - were all able to advance their societies and economic status to that of developed or merging developed status through the use of an R&D-based techno-economic plan, compatible with advanced developed education, technological and industrial systems". As it is well known, many of them were able to realize their nations' dream in spite of many problems and obstacles that confronted some of them during the transformation act. They, the nowadays Arabs, can accomplish the same advanced society status by doing the same - implementation and realization of AU modeled on EU - especially in presence of all present numerous local and foreign stimuli. Amen!

6.5 Establishment of "Arab Union"

"As demonstrated throughout the text, the Arab World is presently divided, more or less, into have and have-not oil rich countries in the ratio of about 31:69%, but because of war conditions in Iraq and the relatively large population to energy income in Algiers, the rich to none rich Arab countries ratio deteriorates down to about 12: 88% (see Chapter 2). By all measures and indices of U.N. and modern developed nations' economy, both segments – oil rich and poor Arab countries - are classified as developing countries. Major reason giving rise to the present situation is the lack of utilization of modern R&D-based techno-economic plans in developing the region's economy. Still, the absence of unity, industrialization and the minimum of cooperation and coordination, are main factors that kept the 20 Arab countries none developed. Furthermore, the region is characterized by the many conflicts, some of which led to local and foreign wars. Very important also, besides that the region is not industrialized and none developed, it is presently highly exposed, mainly because of abundance of oil presence in the region, to major geopolitical and world economic conditions; dominated by major dominant world powers of which the Arab region has been excluded".

To reform and remedy the present unhealthy Arab situation, it was recommended by the authors in their proposal to form an "Arab Union" specifically modeled on EU, which is expected to give AU countries and population similar benefits as those already acquired by the EU model to all the members. The initiative is very much supported by the many local and foreign now persisting and futuristic local and foreign geopolitical and techno-economic stimuli, all of which are now favorable for the formation and implementation of the proposed Arab   Union and the creation of an open Arab common market. We believe no power can prevent them - the Arabs - to undertake the highly beneficial decision's movement. The present 10 Arab Mediterranean membership with 33 other European nations' decision to form the UM was smoothly accomplished without any outside neither interference or any major objection; so why can't the Arab region similarly also smoothly unite, through which they shall progress as proposed by forming AU? What is stopping them - the Arabs - now to unite are: their own hesitancy and indecisive decision, division and lack of coordination among them [4]. **They no longer can continue to claim that other powers are stopping them from implementing the union!!!!** The present case of economy in the Arab World countries as well as in the rest of the world, calls for such an urgent "Arab Union" formation and development; mainly to prevent further regional deterioration, local and foreign disastrous, evil conflicts that force other mighty nations to interfere in Arabs' affairs. The AU formation is also very essential as well as a critical step to be taken quickly by the region in order to meet the needs and demands of the great expected rise in region's population, doubling within the coming two decades. All these liabilities and region's inability to compete on in world markets, again, calls for the same by upgrading of the region to pursue a different techno-economical approach and plan in developing a region that possesses nearly all the potential means, qualities and attributes, potentially qualifying it for an advanced great and outstanding geopolitical and techno-economic status and world's contribution (see prior Section 6.4).

*(**The question** is again and again repeated; for God sake why is not's now possible for the region to accomplish such highly beneficial AU formation and common market's development?)*

The proposal - "Arab Union" specifically designed and modeled on European Union"- formation can be accomplished, as was done by many advanced, progressive regional unions, but in this case specifically as recommended throughout the text by following and limiting the approach to that followed and implemented by the European Union model: **firstly,** by establishing of an "AU" common community free market potentially covering all the 20 contiguous Arab countries with an area of over 12.9 square kilometer, followed **secondly,** by the introduction of large technology transfer industry, effectively fully integrating it at the same time, **thirdly,** with an advanced colossal R&D-based techno-economic development plan, in which **fourthly,** R&D plays a major critical part having proposed expenditure of an up to 5% or more of region's total GDP. **Fifthly:** work on building of an efficient educational system fully compatible and simultaneously integrated with the proposed AU R&D-based techno-economic development plan that shall produce   all the highly skilled technical manpower required to run the plan. The AU itself, **sixthly**: is modeled on the high performance, advanced R&D-based techno-economic development "European Union" plan, which had been successfully functioning over 5 decades. **Seventh**: the approach followed by "European Union", of maintaining the independence of each country and form of government is more than suitable, fitting the Arab states' governments demand for the proposed Arab Union; therefore, the same principle shall be retained and followed in the structuring of the proposed "Arab Union".

Through out the ages, a variety of unions have being established among the world nations, some were of political, others of economical, or techno-economical nature, while still others led to a complete unification or federation of these nations and states to complete union within one country or united region. The proposed "Arab Union" Initiative, which is a techno-economical and in a way also introduces political developmental union, involving potentially the unity of all Arab countries under the proposed "Arab Union", should follow the same approach as that used in forming other successful now working unions and common markets. For the many reasons already given in Section 6.1, the EU model was accurately and conveniently selected to follow in establishment and development of AU.

Although World War II was disastrous to Europe and rest of the world, one of its greatest outcome and therefore advantages was the very wise decision of replacement of colonial, super nationalistic rule, dominating then prior to the war, which also was main reason for it, with development of new world order including the establishment of the "European Union". The various consecutive events and steps taken during the formation of EU were sufficiently detailed in Chapter 5, Section 5.2; their study should benefit and help in founding of the proposed Arab neighbor on: how to perform and implement the AU proposed task and plan of action. To facilitate the task, it was further recommended to pursue the many EU steps and process formation/development with the proposed EU aiding AU as an honest, needed advisor and broker as well. Such an approach will not only speedup the AU establishment process but shall also allow the Arabs to avoid many unnecessary, costly steps in performing the union. Information is also to be collected and thoroughly examined on how other highly successful regional unions, such as the GCC and the Arab League experiences in the running, operation, programming, monitoring, as well as methods and plans used in optimizing the over all union's system performance, evaluation and upgrading. Selective, highly developed union national/regional international programs are also to be investigated and concerned parties consulted to aid in smooth, efficient start of the proposed Arab Union.

Initially, the AU initiation step can be started by a special Arab group favoring the formation of the Arab Union, as was done similarly in 1957 by a special EU European group. Several ways can be followed in accomplishing the proposed "AU" Initiative. It can be started and sponsored, for example, by the already established 6 member GCC Arab Gulf or the 5 member UAM North African Arab countries. In view of the recent formation of "Union of Mediterranean" Nations, wherein the heads/high ranked representatives of 10 Arab Mediterranean countries literally ran to attend Paris Summit and swiftly approved "UM'"s establishment, make us postulate and believe that the Arab mode toward unity has finally and very drastically changed. The same hypothesis made us assume that the way these Arab Mediterranean countries, approved the "UM" formation, the same approach can be followed in sponsoring and cultivation of the proposed "AU" Initiative's formation and why not!

The very weak incoherent function so far of the 5 member "UAM" union, itself, strangely modeled on EU, does not provide strong support for them to lead such a role. Since the start of its founding only a few Summit meetings were held, followed by the recently held meeting in which they were encouraged by the visit of U.S.A. Secretary of States [September 7, 2008], who requested and recommended   to strengthen and speed up the union function and forget all their disputes, mainly borders disputes by annexation of Western Sahara land to Morocco. This case leaves only the 6 member GCC union or the 10 Arab Mediterranean countries, to lead in initiating the move of AU formation with the assistance of the Arab League and definitely the EU technical aid as well.

The new great capital wealth and the good progress accomplished so far by "GCC" union, their continuous annual Summit meetings are convincing factors that preferably GCC assumes the responsibility, endorsement and sponsorship of "AU" initiation and complete AU formation. The present rush of many Arab and none Arab citizens to have working entrée to the GCC's rich market still constitute another major cause for this wise selection. This conclusion is further supported by the present strong desire of many other Arab countries, such as Yemen, to join GCC union. Furthermore, we assumed that part of GCC great wealth can be used to cover and aid the cost of the AU formation, and why not? (During the First ever Arab Economic Summit Conference in Kuwait, January 2009, three GCC countries alone -Saudi, Kuwait and Qatar- pledged a total of $1.75 billions for the reconstruction of war destroyed Gaza as a result of Israeli-Gaza war). Such a move by "GCC" and their endorsement and responsibility for AU initiation and development shall give them as already mentioned the credit for the renewal of advancement and reawakening of the Arab world, similar to that achieved by their - GCC-Arabian Peninsula ancestors about 14 centuries ago. They then led the Arabs eventually to the creation of the Arab Civilization Golden Age Era as well as the creation of the present Arab World (for more detail on this issue see Chapters 1 and 5, Section 5.3).

Let us remind GCC that unlike the presently enormously rich Gulf Arab GCC states (see Chapter 2, Section 2.1), the 7th century Arabs were extremely poor, but highly motivated, stimulated by the strength of their message (see Chapter 1). Could GCC Arab countries, with their again present fabulous capital riches and their union's progressive accomplishment, be motivated to duplicate the old Arab previous awakening and revival act, returning back to the Arabian Peninsula countries - now GCC countries - the starting and building up of this magnificent, greatly beneficial Arab Union?

The puzzling, very critical and articulate question is: how can one transcript and implant in minds of present GCC's rulers and population (see Reference 4) to accept endorsement and adoption of such a highly motivated, stimulated AU Initiative and message for the initiation and start of this magnificently proposed Arab Union? (May we continue to remind them - the Arabs – of: EU, U.S.A unions, the BRIC group of countries how they progressed through union formation combined with implementing the appropriate techno-economic plan see Section 6.4 of this chapter). It should allow them gain all the earlier mentioned benefits in addition, the move provides them and the rest of the Arabs the complete freedom to travel, work, invest and live peacefully, secure within this huge Arab region. May we remind GCC's that their AU endorsement and development duplicates and simulates the greatest Abbasside's act for establishing of the 'First Golden Age Era Miracle' (750-1300)'? The Abbasside's movements dealt then with revival and use of science, knowledge and know how to enrich then the Arab existing empire together with its huge market; same approach can be utilized by GCC in enriching the present Arab regions. GCC movement shall represent a great advancement for the revival of Arab development of technology and knowledge in the region, for which GCC members will be again: recognized, glorified, acknowledged, accredited and highly appreciated for that great accomplished job. Indeed, the act alone by itself constitutes one of the greatest GCC's accomplishments.

Initiation and sponsoring of AU by GCC, again because of its fabulous capital wealth and experience gained in successfully running GCC, constitute a major stimulus for other Arab countries to join AU as is now wanted by many neighboring Arab States. I am certain; the move will be led first by Yemenis, who as mentioned are now very anxious to join GCC. Definitely the Yamani will be competing with rest of Arab countries including the equally anxious 10 Arab UM member states and rest of Arab countries, racing them at a much greater speed than that very fast speed, which carried them to approve joining UM! We strongly believe that this GCC's endorsement and move once taken shall result in a chain reaction, driving all Arab nations to join without hesitation as AU members. The AU initiation by GCC is very much justified and is as explained earlier the equivalent of the first EU and U.S.A union moves.

As was done by the 6 Western European in sponsoring and developing the EEC and later changed name - three times - eventually to European Union, likewise the 6 GCC unions could lead the Arab community in "Arab Union's" formation and development. As normally done at GCC's scheduled Summits, a pre-held special GCC governments' foreign ministers is convened with the purpose of: first naming of an "AU Formation Committee", consisting of one lead member (and required support staff) per country, to which is added one senior, union's expert (and support staff) from each of Arab League and EU as a none voter advisors.

The first task for the "AU Formation Committee" is the drafting of the AU Charter, **reflecting** the AU's objectives and responsibility; second to recommend future AU's head quarter and Secretariat site; third to develop an initial "Short Term Time Schedule" for the first 2 and 5 years AU action plan and budget; covering essential tasks – programs and projects - to be performed during this "AU Phase 1 Initiation" program. After the approval of these three AU's draft proposals by GCC foreign ministers and heads of GCC's States, work on proposal shall start immediately: implementing the AU proposal, using the selected AU headquarters office.

Initial work of the "AU Formation Committee" shall be performed first on this "Short Term Time Schedule" implementation, with all participants adhering   to time schedule without deviation. Unlike previous no action done previously by the North African countries on developing UAM modeled on EU, this AU establishment act is a very serious task and business that must be fully completely implemented. As was done by EU, proposed programs, projects and interfering problems as well as other issues related to AL's operation, expansion and development are presented to AU then responsible committee, discussed, argued and amicable solution is found, accepted - some are rejected - and implemented. Failure is not to be tolerated, since it will reflect on and affect the whole process. (Remember how efficient were the early Arabs; not only in about 110 years they controlled and run an empire for several centuries from Spain to the borders of China but also they were able to continue maintain their culture and civilization for many centuries including use and maintenance of Arabic in a very huge area). Work by the "AU Formation Committee" and   rest of AU and EU staff then continues on expanding "AU", at a fast pace, to include the rest of all qualified Arab countries, who meet the criteria of AU's charter, laws and regulations. The work involves activity on how to develop AU's implementing techno-economic and industrial status, with special emphasis on: implementation of technology transfer industrial projects, raising the region R&D efforts and expenditure and intensity (at least to minimum of 5% of region's GDP) as well as development of an educational system compatible with regional techno-economical, industrial and science developmental plans to produce the necessary manpower for the plan. The same developmental educational and technological, with special large GCC's aid programs are introduced to less develop, potential AU Arab country members to assist them qualify for AU membership as   was done earlier by EU. The AU efforts shall also define and expand other work to be done by the "AU Formation Committee" including recommendation for future AU work in the upcoming Phase 2.

With the completion of Phase 1 (maximum 2 years), Phase 2 will start calling for the expansion of new permanent AU Secretariat office and their responsibilities; also appointing AU Secretary General, and new AU Operation and Expansion Committee, with the objective of running and operation of AU long term program and its gradual expansion to potentially include all Arab states. Additional laws, regulation, summits and otherwise meetings are held on a frequent basis - and Summits for head of states - to deal with AU upgrading, expansion and introduction of new rules and regulations as well as solving of problems confronting the union development. The permanent AU Secretariat shall draw a long term "AU Time Schedule" with the help of EU and in cooperation with all ex-members of the first AU Formation Committee, some of the latter group may be retained as AU advisers or as part of the new permanent AU Secretariat.

(The above proposed Phase 1 and 2 steps are only preliminary ones, representing a general assumed approach concerned mainly with steps required to initiate and get approval of the process by GCC governments and authorities along with initial programs. From EU and GCC experiences more detailed information and modification of the above proposed plan that lead to a faster AU implementation approach may be introduced and applied in this case. In both the above proposal or modification thereof are applied, but most important is that the Arab Union formation, regardless of approach used, must proceed at a fast pace, since the region needs it now and much more so for the very near future, when the region's present shortages, problems and population are expanding at a fast pace never witnessed before).

6.6 Region must Enhance Pan Arab R&D Efforts

The great surge in energy cost, with the spectacular rise in price of oil from about $30/barrel about 3 years ago, reaching up to about $147.5/ barrel, now less than one half the price (over $65-70 per barrel), caused a huge increase in price of other commodities. It eventually also led to a drastic huge decline in car sale worldwide; initially caused a great decline in sale and production of high gas consumer U.S. Auto - gas guzzler - followed soon after by an also serious decline - less than that of American cars - in car production and sale worldwide. In consequence of this great surge in cost of energy there was a rush by advanced nations to increase R&D expenditure and intensity to find an alternative, affordable energy sources, especially renewable, environmentally friendly energy form. In the same manner, it also sent U.S. and other auto makers worldwide, whose sale was declined, searching R&D to identify new modified cars' engine and design having much higher efficiency and lower gas consumption.

The above R&D efforts were enhanced worldwide to overcome the great surge in the above cost of energy, doubling of food prices (ceareals) and with anticipated rise in world population, the solving of shortages in life essential materials needed for human, animal and plant life. Search for more effective drugs to fight deadly diseases such as aids, also search for new high property materials and processes produced through the new nanotechnology procedure, the increased R&D efforts in   stem cell research now supported by present U.S.A government, the endless R&D innovation processes worldwide to produce new products, drugs, markets and new scientific and technical know how plus many other R&D activities; all these factors enhanced R&D efforts required to solve not only present but also future relevant technical and industrial world problems. For example, we reported that the EU (including all members) goals in Research and Development are projected to achieve by 2010 an R&D intensity of at least 3% of GDP compared to present spending of 1.84% of GDP. South Korea too is to increase R&D spending to reach 5% of GDP by the year 2012 from the present 3%. Furthermore, in both cases two thirds of the R&D expenditure is to be financed by the business sector. U.S., China, Japan   and many other advanced countries follow suit by increasing the R&D's GDP funding ratio.

For the first above case (surge in price of energy), consider the U.S. and other advanced developed nations R&D approach. They all stood up for the challenge by implementing an immediate funding of enlarged R&D and other industrialized efforts, specifically R&D efforts undertaken in solar, wind, clean coal and other alternative, environmentally compatible energy sources. Objective of the R&D work is to solve and find adequate solution to overcome the high cost of energy, with great benefit to the large worldwide consumers. As a result, we now witness a large shift toward increased use of wind mills and solar devices introduced by these countries to combat and lower high cost of energy as well as minimize environmental damage. R&D programs were also directed toward the enhancement of natural gas production while others dealt with the production of clean coal and how to prevent production of harmful emission. Potentially, the R&D move has a great positive effect to world population, but somehow negative effect on the income of oil-rich producing nations; although beneficial to preserve the diminishing non-renewable world oil supplies, which are the essential starting materials for the production of petrochemical materials.

By comparison, this awareness and commendable efforts did not activate or move the non-developed nations, including Arab World, to perform the same act. It completely fails the latter group to alert them to the ability, great power and benefits of this extremely important R&D approach in solving their severe, stagnant problems. Consider as an example what the developing Arab region can accomplish using the R&D approach in development of their resources, particularly in solving their very serious shortages in human life-essential materials-water and food production.

The Arab World countries are the world's poorest in fresh water supply from natural resources, coupled with it severe shortage in food production, which now they purchase from world markets. As predicted by each and every Arab country both shortages are presently among the most serious and damaging problems confronting the Arab World population. Problems will be much more exaggerated by the Arab World accelerated rise in population number, now over 329 million, which is expected to rise at an alarming growth rate pace to double their present number in about two decades. On the other hand, they - the Arab countries - have a total of about 23,000 km of coastal area bordering two oceans and three large seas. Of total Arab land of 5 million square miles only about 715,000 square miles - 13% of the total area - is presently utilized as arable, populated land; the remaining portion (87%) is desert. According to U.N., nearly about 50% of world population is expected to live within 50 and 60 miles from the sea within the coming two decades. If fresh water can be made available from the sea at an affordable cost, a huge area of land is likely or could potentially be added - up to 718,750 square miles - to the presently utilized arable Arab land, potentially doubling the arable land area. The large growth rate in region's population requires a matching expansion in Arab land, which all can be managed and solved by use of seawater desalination technology, to extract fresh water in abundance at an affordable cost from the many great oceans and seas surrounding their shores [19].

Presently, the world's production of fresh desalinated water is in excess of 46 million cubic meters per day (m3/d). The waste water from this desalinated water can be further treated locally at the site at a further reduced price. About 60% of this sum is extracted from seawater feed; majority of it produced in the dry, oil-rich Arab Gulf countries, with lesser quantities produced in Libya and Algiers and very little in Iraq. The rest of Arab countries, although they badly need fresh desalinated seawater, they unfortunately can't afford it. To make it affordable requires further R&D desalination development to reduce production cost [19]. With the availability of water from the well-be further developed SWRO and thermal seawater desalination processes along with technology improvement of food production processes and the coastal regions mild climate, should allow for planting of more than one crop per year, helping in meeting the region's future generation demand for reducing both shortages- water and food production.

*Appropriate present and future Arab World's regional planning and strategy should give this important R&D development of SWRO and thermal plus different processes their top and utmost regional cooperative priority planning as much as that given by developed countries to the above energy solution and other R&D issues. **But** would they - the Arabs World countries - do jointly develop the necessary R&D technology to solve this very serious life-essential necessity, stressing technical problems; or continue waiting for advanced nations to perform the task?* Presently, these foreign R&D developers in advanced countries *are not in a great rush to undertake the action, simply because the process is not a high profit one compared to performing other much higher profitable R&D works; they shall continue to wait until the economic profit opportunity allows. Meanwhile many Arabs will die of thirst and hunger while waiting for their government to provide them with this life essential matter. Simply this detrimental act would have been adequately avoided and correctly solved by Arabs conducting and developing the proper R&D not only for seawater desalination processes but also for the treatment of waste water produced after its use. The desalinated fresh water can be produced from the abundant seas bordering their land in abundance at affordable cost as proposed by the writer [19]!*

Like many other developing nations, the Arab world countries in order to solve the above and much more other problems are in a critical need of massive R&D technology to solve the above shortages. Their solution can be found in raising their R&D efforts, intensity and expenditure. Besides finding solution to the above shortages - in human life-essential materials- there are many compelling needs for increased R&D work to raise the region's population's standard of living and technology status. There exists also a need of high urgency and priority for the region industrialization and technology development. With the availability of AU applying R&D-based techno-economic plan, subsidized with large R&D funding of about 5% of the region GDP, the Arab World can also conduct R&D work to solve their population's severe low income and high unemployment rate. What the Arab countries need now is to build and strongly stimulate the sad case of Arab R&D efforts to give them the capability in various development fields to solve their stagnant technology and shortages' problems, while employ for the region's development the thousands of idle or highly under utilized university graduates.

The rich part of Arab community believes they can afford to buy the technology products and need not worry about technology development- Too much hassle!! Time for this attitude to change; they the Arabs have the capital and manpower to perform the urgently needed work; yet they continue to ignore the benefits of R&D in solving such relevant, high priority problems to their region. They continue to export their main wealth – capital and potentially skilled man power! Time to wake-up to recognize the great, tremendous benefits of R&D in lifting up nations' progress and technology development as was done by the entire advanced, developed world, who by the way are now much richer than the rich Arabs. If Arab World countries want to improve their techno-economic situation and upgrade their status, there is no way that can surpass the proposed Arab Union in timely achieving this goal and the raising of their R&D efforts? Time also for the Arab population - both government and private - to stand up for the challenge and to cover region's shortages; to overcome petty problems and differences that kept them disunited and also to satisfy poor Arab population's (about 88%) needs for higher, improved living standards, the way advanced nations now maintain. Again, the process is urgently required; the alternative to this option as indicated is poverty, dying of thirst and hunger which no one wants - government or private.

The region continues to severely suffer from a lack of Arab nations' R&D spending in its various sectors. All R&D efforts are government sponsored and funded; nearly none of it is sponsored or funded by the absent but very important private enterprise companies, or the region's dominating family owned businesses. The sad R&D efforts and funding as stated is extremely low, about 0.2 % of region's GDP compared up to about 3.86% and 4.95% in year 2005 for Sweden and Israel, respectively. Chapters 3 and 4 detail the GDP% funded by nations worldwide.

The present section provides a summary list of R&D actions to be done jointly by the region to promote and develop a so far very much neglected regional, yet extremely potentially important Arab R&D efforts (see Chapter 3, Section3.1 to 4). The establishment of AU with major centralized activity on use of R&D will definitely improve R&D's regional capability and shall provide them the power to overcome present and future problems confronting them. These strongly recommended and proposed common pan Arab R&D measures, which are urgently required by the region, are:

1. The optimal most satisfying effective method that should allow for a speedy rise and catch-up of Arab region' industrial and economic developmental efforts as well as R&D capability is the formation and development and implementation of Arab Union. The AU plan, as proposed, is an R&D dependent and centered; wherein R&D constitutes the back bone and corner stone for it to succeed in development of AU overall techno-economic, scientific and technological activities. This R&D-based techno-economic developmental plan should be fully integrated with a compatible educational system to produce the required manpower to successfully operate it. Such an AU R&D plan,

as proposed, is generously funded- by at least 5% or more of Arab region' GDP- and is supported by nations' industrialization. It is presently rigidly applied without exception by all advanced developed and emerging nations.

2. Another obvious approach of increasing investments and Involvement in R&D is done by allocating a much larger percentage of Arab nations' GDP income toward R&D efforts, as being done by advanced nations (see for detail Chapters 3 and 4). This is partially attempted now by the Saudi Arabian government. The Kingdom as mentioned is to increase research and development spending to 2.5% of GDP from its relatively low ratio of 0.2-0.5% of GDP, for a total of over SR 32 billion ($8.6 billion) as part of its 20-year National Science and Technology Plan [20]. The suggested period is quite lengthy, and the % is low, if the country desires to make-up for the earlier lost progress and catch-up with advancement acquired by an already high economy nations. To emphasize the GDP ratio should be highly raised to reach about 5% in a very few years, not to exceed 5 years. This is very essential in order for the country to catch up in this very critical and important field of science and techno-economic development, particularly with the expected large increase in population, doubling in about two decades. In spite of that the move, the plan is still considered to be positive and in the right direction, however, Arab world needs to fast-tracked their efforts to address the many   pressing R&D requirements of the region.

3. Another approach would be for the economies of the Arab World - rich and poor - to effectively pool and merge their R&D resources and efforts in one large fund so as to create a highly effective "Pan Arab R&D Fund" to push and advance the region as a whole in building and advancing their industry and economy, concentrating on high priority R&D critical problems, such as life-essential maters of water and food shortages plus health, industrial, scientific and other many problems. The fund, as was proposed by the writer way back in1967 [3], would effectively organize such investments without unnecessary duplication of effort within the region. Cross-mergers between leading technology industries and companies are now important for Arab industry to transfer raw materials into high value products, such as the: petroleum, phosphate, building material, etc. R&D efforts are also to cover many other activities, especially in developing   new industries that the region now lacks such as : food industry, textile, water treatment, pharmaceutical, energy, car manufacturing; plus high-tech companies in electronic, information technology, nanotechnology, stem cell research plus many, many others industries that the Arab region presently lacks. They have a long industry list, especially high tech ones, to catch-up with other advanced developed nations/regions of the world.

4. The recent $10 billion endowment introduced by "Sheikh Mohammed bin Rashid Al-Maktoum Foundation" constitutes another means of promoting R&D efforts in the

Arab World, although it is not a completely R&D designed. The foundation has set goals to promote human development in the region with emphasis on R&D, science and technology development [21]. Other R&D endowments, needs to be developed and encouraged, which can effectively serve in the same manner as used in developed World.

5. There are huge number of such R&D and other charitable organization in advanced world nations. By comparison, the Arab charitable Foundations in R&D are by far much less in number and activities than their counterpart in advanced and emerging developed nations, although one major act in Islam is strongly advocate and emphasize R&D and charity donation. One of the greatest donations is that which provides greatest benefits to largest members of a nation/region, which is achieved (see Section 5.3.1) by the development of nations economy through the first four Islamic principles ''Read, Write and perform R&D''. So, why does not the Arab world have such charities working toward this goal ''Read, Write and perform R&D''? True many charitable person' or family organizations are engaged in religious charitable deeds, such as building mosques, why not to extend their activity to cover also R&D work, especially when the action serves all, was emphasized in the above first message in Islam?

6. Elsewhere, in developed countries, R&D funding of about 60-70% or more is contributed by the private enterprise sector. The present contribution to R&D by the Arab private sector is nil, extremely negligible, mainly because of the absence of this sector in the Arab market, which, to a great extent as repeatedly emphasized, is family controlled, limited only to each country's borders. Their main concern is trade and commercial transactions mainly with company outside the region. So far these family businesses failed to develop R&D work. In order to boost the contribution of the private sector R&D efforts, the private enterprise companies - local or foreign - must be encouraged to spread all over across the Arab land, covering the entire region, with full guarantee and security of investment, industrial and distribution-wise and not to continue remained localized. Various incentives for R&D investment within the region, such as: financial subsidies, access to required high skilled R&D foreign labor, joint R&D work and permits, protection and guarantee of intellectual property laws and benefits gained thereof, etc, are to be offered by the Arab governments. Equally important, is to follow the advanced nations system in attracting R&D scientists and engineers, providing them with all the necessary motives and attractions, to join and participate in development of Arab R&D programs, maintaining their rights to match and to equal those rights granted to the locals.

7. The Arab world countries need to enhance, develop as well as maintain qualified and skill R&D manpower resources. This can be achieved by raising the relevant Pan R&D institutes and AU establishment in the region as was recommended under items 1

and 2 above. Much higher Scientific and technological education in both quality and quantity combined with relevant R&D work at the university must be introduced and heavily subsidized. Many of advanced and emerging nations realized the effectiveness of such manpower to the revival and expansion of their techno-economic, scientific and market place and therefore introduced variety of special efforts and programs to encourage potential researchers to join in great number (see Chapter 4, Section 4.1; also for comparison of R&D researchers in Arab world and that in advanced countries see Section 6.3 of this chapter).

8. For guidance and support in this R&D field, however, the Arabs are to seek the technical aid, services and proper advice from advanced countries, in particular USA, EU, China and Japan and other R&D advanced communities. These advanced nations shall be requested to aid the region on how to accelerate the R&D development and in consequence techno-economic activity within the region. Definitely, they all shall emphasize much higher level and funding of R&D institutes, combined with much greater involvement of Universities, governments and free enterprise companies in this very important field of national and R&D techno-economic activity. Definitely and of course too they shall strongly support the founding and development of the R&D-centered, the proposed magnificent "Arab Union".

...   .

References:

1. UM, Mediterranean countries to forge union, 2008, 07,13, http://news.xinhuanet. com

2. Union for the Mediterranean, from Wikipedia, the Free Encyclopedia.

3. Dr. Ata M. Hassan, L.S. Bitar and Dr. M.K. Hamid, Development of a Pan Arab R&D Institutes and Industrial Technology, 1967.

4. Emil J. Kirchner, "The European Union as a Model for Regional Integration: The Muslim World and Beyond," Jean Monnet/Robert Schuman Paper Series Vol.6 No.1 January 2006.

5. The United Nations Development Program (UNDP) released the Arab Human Development Report 2002, July 2, 2002. (The report, compiled by a "group of distinguished Arab intellectuals" led by Egyptian statistician Nader Fergany)

6. Subtitled "Building a Knowledge Society, United Nations Development Program published its second Arab Human Development Report On Oct. 20 04.

7. Science and Tech Science and Tech Publication: Zenit.org, Advocating an Arab Aggiornamento, Reforms Outlined to Help Islamic Culture Open Up to the Modern, November 15, 2003,

8. Human Development in the Arab World: Islam is Blocking Progress, by John L. Perkins, these problems has been depicted recently in the Arab Human Development Report (AHDR 2003), produced by a group of Arab specialists for the United Nations Development Program This is a follow-up of a similar report made in 2002,

9. How the Arabs Compare Arab Human Development Report 2002, Internet.

10. Human Development in the Arab World: Islam is Blocking Progress, by John L. Perkins, these problems has been depicted recently in the Arab Human Development Report (AHDR 2003), produced by a group of Arab specialists for the United Nations Development Program. This is a follow-up of a similar report made in 2002,

11. Study Warns of Stagnation in Arab Societies, By Barbara Crossette, <u>New York Times</u>, July 2, 20, the <u>Arab Human Development Report 2002</u>,

12. Wagdy Swahili, Brain drain threatens future of Arab science, June 2004, Source: SciDev.Net

13. **Wasim Maziak**[*] ,Performing your original search, Arab World spending on R D, in Science will retrieve GLOBAL VOICES OF SCIENCE:

14. The Oxford History of Islam, Editor John L. Esposito, Oxford University press, 149 pages, with 15 contributors.

15. Patricia S. Daniel and Stephen G. Hyslop, Almanac of World History, Library of Congress Publication, 2003.

16. Philip K. Hitti, The History of the Arabs, New York, Palogrove McMillan, 2002, 10th Edition, 822 pages, first edition published 1937.

17. Albert Hourani, Arab History, Oxford Press, December 2003.

18. South Korea, from Wikipedia, the Free Encyclopedia.

19. Ata M. Hassan, Blue Revolution, San Diego, California, U.S.A, 2008.

20. Saudi Arabia will spend over SR 32 billion ($8.6 billion) on research and development as part of its 20-year National Science and Technology Plan, *Arab News* reported today.

21. Sheikh Mohammed bin Rashid Al Maktoum launches foundation promote human development with DHS 37 billion endowment "Mohammed Bin Rashid Al Maktoum Foundation" to develop future leaders and create knowledge-based society in the region,Jordan,2; also Loai Naomani, $10 billion, May 21,2007.

22. Jamal Abel Nasser, UAR Formation, Wikipedia, the Free Encyclopedia.

23. -GLOBAL VOICES OF SCIENCE: Science in the Arab World: Vision of Glories Beyond, Middle East Quarterly, Fall 2002.

24. .*Nature* **444**, 35-36 (2 November 2006): 10.1038/444035, Islam and science: Where are the new patrons of science?

25. Womengateway.com> Business > Features , Investing in Research and Development, By Mo Fakhro

26. Arabic text of Arab League Summit Meeting Recommendation, Doha, Qatar, March 2009.

Conclusion

By the end of the disastrous World War II (1945), which caused the death of over 67 million humans, drastic changes occurred in world political and economic order. The world nations' concept of colonialism and super nationalism, which were practiced prior to the war by both the European and Japanese's powers, were completely discarded. They were replaced by a new geopolitical and economic world order granting freedom and independence to all previously colonized nations. Great emphasis and concern were also directed on "how to fix and revive the nations' world economy by shifting nations/regions' effort toward the revival and development of their pre- and post-war techno-economic status"; the change covered either nations that were already or many newly independent states.

The post-war drove 6 Western European war damaged nations to start first, as early as 1957, the formation and development of EEC market, which eventually developed into the present "European Union", with 31 European independent member countries; total population over 500 millions. In order to develop its economy at a respectable, relatively high rate, EU have implemented over the last 5 decades a strongly, rigidly adhered to R&D –based techno –economic and industrial developmental plans, combined with massive Industry, technology and supported with well –defined, highly –focused R&D constituted the backbone to these advancements. All – these advanced techno-economic plans - were in conformity with other plans then used by advanced nations, some in European countries but mostly in U.S.A, which they – EU - then greatly admired their richness and successful approach of free enterprise open market (for more detail on initiation, development and present status of EU, see Chapter 5, Section 5.2).

The techno-economic and social welfare's concern of many newly independent governments of East Asia Pacific Ridge countries plus other nations elsewhere led them also, some as early as 1960, to follow then the same advanced nations' successful techno-economic plans, which eventually made them shift from previously underdeveloped to now highly develop nations or emerging nations' status. The group included South Korea, Taiwan, Singapore, Hong Kong, Malaysia plus BRIC's group of nations plus many others in Europe (see Chapters 3 and 4). The shift from have-not to have, rich ,high-tech nations was achieved in spite of many problems confronting many of them during the shift process, such as poverty, some with initial military rule plus many other problems. These many countries along with EU realized their **nations' dream** by strictly following and rigidly apply the same advanced nations' successful highly progressive, greatly rewarding R&D-based techno-economic plans.

Against the progress of above groups of nations/regions that rigidly used R&D-based techno- economic approach, many others failed to pursue the same above trend. This group included a great number of countries: the Spanish speaking countries of South and Central American Continents, African and parts of Asian countries, especially many Muslim and Arab countries plus others. They were left behind, underdeveloped with little progress, non-industrialized, many remained in same conditions as they were in the past several decades. This contradictory condition gave rise to the observed great differences in overall status of advanced and none advanced states and the world's division into fortunate have (developed, rich) and unfortunately have-not (developing, relatively poor) nations, with great difference in GDP per capita income(for more detail on this transformation process see Chapters 4; for the critical and very essential role of R&D in development and change of techno-economic status of advanced and emerging nations and how their negligence kept others underdeveloped, see Chapters 3 and 4).

The above several examples teach us that:

- In order for a developing country/region shifts its techno-economic status to developed one, it must rigidly perform the same transformation steps as were already done by the above nations- U.S.A, Japan, EU, the Asia Pacific Ridge countries, the BRIC's group – Brazil, Russia, India and China - of nations, many countries in Europe plus many others - now all advanced or emerging countries.

- Only through use and rigid, routine implementation of this advanced nations techno-economic plan, these nations were able to advance and progress. Neither democracy nor supportive religious attitudes, although may help but as frequently believed by many, were not essential, necessary conditions for their techno-economic progress. China's achievement, now second richest world country in both total GDP and R&D spending, was achieved in spite of absence of so-called democracy, in presence of military rule and one single communist party system.

- Additionally, these cases teaches us too that division of nations into develop and undeveloped is not a steady permanent state; rather it can be drastically changed up or down as demonstrated above by following or departure from a rigid implementation of advanced nations' approach (for more detail on transformation to developing or developed nations' status, see Chapters 3 and 4).

- Furthermore, present world techno-economic situation teach us that Government's tolerance is strongly enhanced by good progressive economy; meanwhile absence of such factor generates the case of intolerance and disorder now observed among many nations, regardless of governments' form. For the latter condition, the present world recession is expected to spark large global unrest. To avoid such fate, the advanced together with emerging nations of the world must honestly and truly cooperate collectively aid poor nations; the rich helping the poor on developing and maintaining a healthy strong world's economies and order.

- The same concept led us too to initiate our present proposal: "how to change developing nations' techno-economic world order: from have-not, poor, underdeveloped to have, rich, develop nations' status". The present book details the transformation process, utilizing only one case for illustration, whose trend was also generalized to cover other candidate cases.

The proposal - R&D–based techno-economic, educational nations' transformation formula, recipe - described in the book is designed as pointed out in Summary Section to assist the willing, determined but now underdeveloped nations/regions of the world catch up with developed status ones, the way it was done above by many others who followed the advanced nations' techno-economic plan. The proposal constitutes an ideal techno-economic model and plan to follow and pursue by the less fortunate developing nations/regions. This achievement allowed EU - as well as other nations that successfully applied the plan - a super model to be applied by many would-be prime candidate regions, which are determined to with the objective: of shift their present developing region to a healthy developed status.

Among the world nations/regions, there are definitely many qualified to apply the above selected super EU model, but by far "its neighbor the Arab region" is now more fit than many others as a primary candidate to subscribe to this proposed EU's model; with the successful outcome of initiating and developing of an "Arab Union" specifically and purposely modeled on EU was preferably selected as the AU model. The selection was based on EU's great success, proximity and previous dealing and exchange of culture and partial sharing of rule of regions plus other factors. The EU transformation model was employed throughout the book to illustrate how it can be applied to AU and further how the process too can be generalized to cover other world qualified transformation cases- nations/regions- that already fit the shift and the transformation criteria.

The ultimate goal of Arab Union's founding and development is outlined in Summary Section of the book. Problems facing Arab world (equally facing other developing nations) are mainly economical in nature, requiring economical as well as political solutions that allows the countries to overlook their present petty disputes; mainly political, and personal self-interest conflicts. The presently friendly relationship that now exists between EU and Arab region countries can simplify the transformation process as demonstrated by seeking EU aid as an active involved advisor in catalyzing AU's as it already did catalyze the Arab-European "Union of the Mediterranean (UM)". The proposal's choice – AU formation modeled on EU - is strongly supported by the same factors and stimuli again as given elsewhere in the book, especially under "The Summary Section". Briefly the choice gives the region   greater share of world trade and free political and economic stance in face of dominating world powers; provides it peace and security, overcoming many of its present conflicts and problems as well as it gives the region the power of contributing to world knowledge and science. Founding of AU is anticipated to create a vast and open Arab common free enterprise market; most important, it shall maintain each AU member country independent retaining same form of government as it is now, which is also in conformity with present demands of all Arab governments and rulers without exception.

Modeling of AU on EU made it essential to compare the Arab and EU during two different eras at their best unionized and worst situation without a union (for more detail see the book's Chapter 5 and also the Summary Section). Specifically, the case compares the EU highly developed status post EU formation (1957- present) to EU status prior to its establishment during the period (1800-1945) of an imperial colonizing, super nationalistic, divided states' system. By comparison the glorious past of a united region covering and ruling an extensive huge area empire, consisting of advanced society engaged in developing science, knowledge and know how during their Arab Golden Age Era unity (750- 1300) is compared to the present (1945 to present) 20 un-unionized, divided Arab world countries, all currently classified as underdeveloped. About 88% are now poor Arab countries, having low GDP population's per capita income and only 12% oil-rich with high per capita GDP income. Most of them none cooperative and non-competitive countries, lacking in R&D, techno-economic and scientific development, their majority are suffering from poverty and conflicts. Arab world needs to be fast –tracked in many fields and efforts to address the region's pressing poverty needs as well as to catch –up with other advanced nations and to provide the region the ability to avoid future severe problems arising from the soon doubling of present population" (for more detail on the subject see Chapters 3 and 4).

Details related to the proposed steps and approach to be undertaken to successfully implement the proposed "Arab Union" modeled on "European Union" are discussed in detail in Chapter 6 and other parts of the book as well. Finally, analogous to the first founding in 1957 of the six Western European nations of the EEC, followed then over the last 5 decades by gradually developing it to its present European Union status, the Arab countries can similarly and smartly, duplicate the act by the initiation of the six member GCC Arab Gulf union with the help and advice of the Arab League and "EU" aid as an advisor (for detail on AU establishment and development see Chapter 6, Section 6.5). The GCC's accomplished good progress combined with its present vast wealth more than qualifies it to lead the Arab World in initiation and completion of this great task. Without a stressing harmful monetary finance, GCC can confidently complete the union, gradually expanding AU to include the rest of Arab nations. We are very much certain that AU sponsoring and endorsement by GCC constitute a major stimulus to rush the Yemenis- who were always very anxious to join GCC- racing the Arab Mediterranean and the rest of Arabs countries to follow suit in joining AU. So, why does not GCC initiate this great, highly beneficial AU act; get the credit and share the enormously anticipated progress and wealth of the region while at the same time maintaining each Arab government' form and independence and wealth as well? As their great, but then poor GCC's ancestors are accredited with the start and development of the great empire, eventually led to the "First Arab Golden Age of Knowledge Miracle (750 –1300)", the present oil –rich GCC Arabs shall also receive the credit and glory of help in performing the present "Second Arab Union's Knowledge Miracle". Amine!

... ...

About The Authors

Dr. Ata M. Hassan, a recipient of many international awards, was born in Halhoul-Hebron, Palestine where he received his primary and high schooling. He obtained his higher education, in Chemistry and material science in the United States: B.Sc. (1956), Roosevelt University, Chicago, M.Sc. (1958), Ph.D. (1966) both from University of Cincinnati. He has been involved in R&D work for over fifty five years (1953-present); over 27 years in USA and about thirty years were in Arab world, principally in water, seawater desalination and resources, material science and development of technology, cooperating with various well-known global R&D organizations and firms working in the field. His endeavors in R&D began in the U.S. 50 years ago where he garnered the fundamentals of basic and applied research at several esteemed research institutes in U.S. as a researcher and senior research scientist. There, he contributed immensely to several accomplishments and publications in numerous fields of science: polymer and breakthrough in wide line solid state NMR and fermentation control and others.

Within the last 30 years (1976-2006), he repatriated his R&D knowledge and experience to the Middle East, where first he joined Kuwait Institute for Scientific Research (KISR) 1976 to 1985; where he initiated and developed, among other activities, the R&D program in desalination and water reuse, culminating in the well-known Doha Reverse Osmosis Plant (DROP), a $52 million joint project between Kuwait and the federal R&D government of Germany. Besides heading the DROP as general manager actively involved in developing the program and its R&D plan, his work activity at KISR also included the initiation of the Arab Institute for Water Desalination & Resources in 1978 to be developed jointly by the Euro Arab Dialogue nations, along with several other activities, such as the establishment of: Central Analytical Lab, Material Science, Water Desalination Divisions, Physical Testing and thermal insulation energy saving.

Later on, continuing his lifelong aspiration to solve the world's water problems, Dr. Hassan joined and continues working (1988- 2006) with the Saline Water Conversion Corporation (SWCC) R&D Center, Saudi Arabia. The extensive research performed at SWCC has led to the groundbreaking invention "developments of new seawater desalination process"; resulting in the introduction of several dual- and tri-hybrid seawater desalination processes utilizing nano-filtration (NF) as a pretreatment method coupled with conventional seawater desalination process systems. The superior NF pretreatment process changes the seawater feed chemistry, performing a breakthrough that made it possible to overcome many of the major problems - bio-fouling, lowering of total dissolved salt (TDS), removal of hardness salts and allowing thermal seawater desalination processes at higher top brine temperature (TBT) - encountered in the various conventional seawater desalination processes. All the hybrids were successfully tested and evaluated on a pilot, demonstrated and commercial plants. The commercial NF-SWRO plant resulted in an over 42% increase in fresh water product yield and over 56% of water recovery ratio, wherein the water yield is doubled, when utilizing the already verified optimal design operating each of the NF and SWRO units in fully integrated two stage hybrid (NF2-SWRO2 and NF2-MSFD) and tri-hybrid (NF2-SWRO2_reject- Thermal) . The new desalination process along with the various hybrids has earned worldwide patents and numerous awards and acclaims from both the scientific and commercial desalination societies.

With the world now experiencing a severe shortage in fresh water supplies and in consequence shortage in food production, the author felt obliged, especially with the poor, that the world community, rich and poor must find technical solutions to help avert the future shortage in two human life-essentials, fresh water and food. Based on his extensive R&D experience, and results obtained by others through use of R&D technology, Dr. Hassan introduced the Blue Revolution (BLRV) concept to develop, through proposed R&D work, seawater desalination processes at the proposed R&D BLRV institutes, to produce fresh water from seawater in sufficient large quantities at affordable cost, and avail the same to whoever needs it to solve the present global water and food shortages. The Blue Revolution Book (2006) describes how this proposal can be done. The Blue Revolution foundation home is the City of San Diego, CA. Presently in the progress and negotiation stage is developing of R&D partnership with others.

In 1967, while working in USA as a senior R&D scientist, Dr. Hassan jointly with others prepared a proposal that dealt with the introduction and implementation of a Pan-Arab R&D Initiative, with the goals and objectives of developing the Arab region's technology, industry and overall economy as done elsewhere by the establishment of various scientific and technological Pan Arab R&D Institutes. The proposal was submitted in the same year -1967- to all and every other Arab embassy in Washington, D.C. Now, it is time for the Arab to wake up, realize their status, and stand up for the 20 century challenge of: replacing the region's failing old economic approach, by considering our present greatly expanded 1967 proposal, for the initiation, implementation and development of a pan "Arab Union"(AU) modeled on the "European Union"(EU). The EU successful formation and implementation over the last 5 decades was one of the greatest advancement and successful techno-economic regional plan done on a grand scale, utilizing an advanced, highly developed R&D-based techno-economic plan, used also by all the other developed nations in development of their now 31 nations' technology, industry and economy. Certainly, the successful story and the great benefits gained thereof by the European member nations and many other world nations strongly deserves the Arab countries recognition to form and develop the "Arab Union" specifically modeled on EU, consequently gaining same benefits as was accomplished by EU neighbor. Definitely, the AU initiative is urgently required "if the Arab World wants to improve their economy and world status from a developing – underdeveloped - to a developed region; overcome many of their common present and future stagnant problems, have their independent thought and decision, establish peace and security throughout the region instead of conflicts, solve their many shortages in life-essential requirements, avoid terror acts, provide employment to their expected highly multiplying population as well as meet population many other modern requirements. The total recipe for the Arab World region, allowing it to transfer their so far developing (under-developed) nation to a developed (advanced) nation's status is fully described in the book together with generalization of the case to other appropriately selected underdeveloped cases. For the Arab world (as well as other qualifying underdeveloped region) no other act can surpass and accomplish mission's goal more than the formation and implementation of the proposed united "AU" modeled on EU.

About Ata M. Hassan, Jr. - Tech Engineer, now a founding partner in a software firm AnalyzeSoft, Inc.

Japanese conglomerates in the East and the birth of Apple Computer on the West - fond memories of a youth offering guiding principles and inspiration for an adulthood. This inspiration, complemented with an early exposure to "high tech" - Heath- kit computer kits, TRS-80 and Apple II computers – provided a foundation for formal advancement in the field of computer engineering at California Polytechnic University. An ensuing knowledge-base of the software engineering lifecycle was attained through award-winning product development initiatives at firms including Xerox, TD Ameritrade, and First American. Combining this experience with an innate entrepreneurial spirit, Analyze Soft, Inc. was launched in December of 2003, with Ata as a founding partner. Analyze Soft's expertise lies in implementing solutions to complex business problems through a unique blend of business, technology, and process. Clients spanning financial to healthcare to non-profit sectors and technologies spanning data warehousing and business intelligence applications to enterprise portals, Analyze Soft continues to develop its services repertoire and is now positioned for the procession into product development and other strategic initiatives. Ata is also the father of four – Aziz, Anouk, Chloe, and Sophie - and husband to a lovely Scottish Highlander, Renee.

The Arab Awakening

The case for transforming a regions' world order from an underdeveloped to a developed status is illustrated through a proposed Arab Union of 20 contiguous Arab countries, 329 million in population, modeled after the European Union consisting of 31 countries and a population exceeding 500 million. This awakening process is anticipated to induce similar techno-economical benefits to the Arab Union as those realized by the EU in its five decades of success. The transformation shall uplift the countries of the Arab Union to an advanced nations status in addition to bringing the region peace and security - avoiding their many present petty conflicts and resulting in a vast free and progressive enterprise for the region of the Arab Union. This model is further generalized to cover other qualified underdeveloped regions that fit the transformation criteria and are sufficiently determined to confront the challenges necessary to change their status from an underdeveloped to a highly developed region - overcoming their many problems currently being witnessed including poverty, disorder and military junta' rule, as was accomplished by the Asian Pacific countries of South Korea, Taiwan, and Singapore along with other emerging and advanced nations such as the U.S., Canada, Israel, China, India, Brazil, Russia and many others.